W9-AEW-626

The Bow and the Lyre: *The Art of Robert Browning*

The Bow and the Lyre

THE ART
OF
ROBERT BROWNING

ROMA A. KING, JR.

Ann Arbor Paperbacks
The University of Michigan Press

First edition as an Ann Arbor Paperback 1964
Copyright © by The University of Michigan 1957
All rights reserved
Published in the United States of America by
The University of Michigan Press and simultaneously
in Toronto, Canada, by Ambassador Books Limited
Manufactured in the United States of America

Designed by George Lenox

TO LUCILLE

Had a spider found out the communion-cup,
Was a toad in the christening-font?

—"Gold Hair"

. . . As with the bow and the lyre, so with
the world: it is the tension of opposing
forces that makes the structure one.

—Heraclitus

I wish to express special thanks to Professors Karl Litzenberg, Austin Warren, and Bennett Weaver, of the University of Michigan. For their sympathetic understanding and patient teaching, which has done so much to shape my thinking about poetry—and especially the poetry of Robert Browning—I am grateful. They were my perceptive critics throughout the time I was writing this book.

I am also indebted to Professors Arthur J. Carr and Frank Huntley of the University of Michigan, to Professor Carl Keppler of the University of Arizona, to Professor Hazel Batzer of Morningside College, to Professor Hyatt H. Waggoner of Brown University for reading and criticizing the manuscript.

Contents

Contents

The Bow and the Lyre: *The Art of Robert Browning*

I

Robert Browning's
Apology

> Mine's freehold, by grace of the grand Lord
> Who lets out the ground here,—my landlord:
> To him I pay quit-rent—devotion;
> Nor hence shall I budge, I've a notion,
> Nay, here shall my whistling and singing
> Set all his street's echoes a-ringing
> Long after the last of your number
> Has ceased my front-court to encumber
> While, treading down rose and ranunculus,
> You *Tommy-make-room-for-your-Uncle us*!
> > —*Pacchiarotto*

Browning's whistling and singing are their own best apology, having safely survived, as the poet foretold, their many critics—friends and enemies alike. Anyone who attempts now to add another to the five thousand titles in the Browning bibliography must do so under threat of the poet's malediction. Yet he can proceed confidently. For even if he fail, the poet will survive; if he should succeed, he may clear away some of the critical accruement of fifty years, permitting the poems once more to speak for themselves. By describing and evaluating a repre-

3

sentative selection of Browning's shorter dramatic poems, I hope to stimulate a fresh, sensitive rereading of his poetry.

Browning has had his detractors, yet he has suffered more from his friends. Much early "criticism" was inspired by the London Browning Society, an organization described by George Bernard Shaw as a "conventicle where pious ladies disputed about religion. . . ." Actually, its initial membership included persons of distinguished ability (G. B. S. himself, for example), but it was soon dominated, as Shaw suggests, by elderly matrons and liberal clergymen less endowed with judgment than enthusiasm. They were, indeed, a prolific group, finding in individual lines and in passages out of context support for such virtues as "faith," "spirituality," and especially "optimism." Proclaiming his inspirational power in monographs and tracts, they shaped the myth of the philosophical and spiritual Browning.[1]

Their dogmatic interest in Browning as a philosopher and teacher discouraged valid literary criticism; their emphasis on the extrapoetic in his work rendered him suspect for a younger generation, less certain than their seniors concerning the whereabouts of God and the rightness of the world. Early in the twentieth century most young readers turned to newer works such as Ezra Pound's *Personae* and, a little later, to T. S. Eliot's *The Waste Land*. Browning fell into disrepute. Recently, however, serious readers and critics have engaged in an attempt to rescue Browning from the reverent hands of early admirers and to establish his position as a poet. Toward this end impressive work has been done.

Distinguished scholars such as William Clyde De-

Vane and Joseph Baker have so effectively combatted the misconception of the Browning societies about Browning's "thought," "philosophy," and "optimism" that to pursue the subject further would be useless repetition. Except in a few remote outposts the Browning societies have been routed. There remains, however, a need for a close critical study of the poems themselves, surprisingly little having been attempted up to now. In fact, the most penetrating critical appraisals of Browning have appeared incidentally in works of general criticism. Ezra Pound proclaims *Men and Women* the most interesting poems of the Victorian period, and throughout his work makes perceptive statements about Browning's functional use of structural devices, notably diction and rhythm.[2] Ford Madox Ford once remarked, "After all, the English poet that matters two pence is Browning." [3] He commends Browning for not considering "verse writing as something apart from life, form, and language," [4] emphasizing particularly Browning's contribution to twentieth-century poetry in form and diction. He makes the point that Browning attempts to invent a new verse form for each of his "varying mental phases." [5]

Including Browning with Nietzsche, Dostoevsky, and Blake in what he calls his personal four-star constellation, André Gide is helpful in suggesting that Browning's *âme élastique* permits him to assume temporarily the role of a character without writing confessional literature.[6] For "The Lost Leader," he says, Wordsworth "served Browning only as a pretext, his falling away only as a starting-point, for a poem; one more opportunity for Browning to depersonalize himself in order to put himself momentarily into someone else." [7]

These insights—scattered throughout the works of Pound, Ford, and Gide—into Browning's dramatic method, his *âme élastique*, his functional use of structural devices to convey meaning, his formal and linguistic contribution to English poetry, are, it seems to me, perceptive. One wishes that either Pound, Ford, or Gide had undertaken to write a formal critical evaluation of Browning's poetry.

It is not my purpose to provide a handbook for the whole of Browning's poetry. Rather, I should like to suggest a critical approach to his work and to describe some of its distinguishing characteristics. I prefer working closely with the poetry itself. It is neither possible nor necessary, however, to discuss all of Browning's poems. My purpose is best served by a group small enough to be studied intensively, and at the same time inclusive enough to represent Browning fairly.

All his works are not of equal value, and patently I should not wish, even if my purpose were more inclusive, to defend everything he wrote, for reasons which I shall offer. Briefly, I conclude that his poetic career reached a height during the period beginning in the late forties and terminating with *The Ring and the Book*. There is, nevertheless, a unity in all his work. The earlier poems, particularly *Sordello*, suggest virtues which he had to cultivate (objectivity; close correlation between thought, emotion, and expression; compactness; irony); *Pauline*, the weaknesses which he had to overcome (subjectivity, intellectual and emotional vagueness, verbosity, sentimentality).

Although Browning wrote some good poems in his old age, it seems to me that after *The Ring and the Book* there is an over-all decline in the merit of his work. Certainly, he continued to experiment, sometimes employing structural devices that are boldly effective. His difficulty, however, was other than structural. He succumbed to Victorian expectations that their poets perform as prophets, and he did not fill the prophetic role well. In contrast to his earlier work, his later is too often emotionally deficient and conceptually overladen. Its quantities of thought are not sufficiently realized poetically.

In his earlier work, his weakness takes the form of one extreme, and in his later, that of another; during the middle period, however, he achieves artistic balance. The poems from this period, then, provide a perspective from which one can, looking backward and forward, view the whole of Browning's work; consequently, I find them most appropriate for my study. I have selected specifically five poems: "Andrea del Sarto," "Fra Lippo Lippi," "The Bishop Orders His Tomb," "Bishop Blougram's Apology," and "Saul."

"Andrea del Sarto" and "Fra Lippo Lippi" are primarily concerned with art, "Bishop Blougram's Apology" and "Saul" with religion—subjects which provide a suggestive approach to Browning's interests. The first two are further related by their Renaissance background. It seems appropriate that these sets of poems be used in pairs and connected by a fifth, "The Bishop Orders His Tomb," which has a Renaissance background and is concerned in a general way with both art and religion. Thus, I account for the order in which the poems appear here.

With one exception they are dramatic monologues. "Saul" is a dramatic narrative related in retrospect by David, a participant in the poem's action. From yet another point of view, "Andrea del Sarto," "Fra Lippo Lippi," and "The Bishop Orders His Tomb" are psychological character studies; "Bishop Blougram's Apology" is dramatic argumentation; "Saul" is narrative didacticism.

These, I believe, sufficiently represent Browning's interests and techniques to provide, in addition to materials for a close analysis, a basis upon which to generalize about Browning's art in the shorter dramatic poems. I propose first to analyze and evaluate each poem as a self-contained work, generalizing about the whole body only incidentally, and finally reversing emphasis to discuss Browning's technique generally, referring only incidentally to the specific works.

To provide a perspective for the following chapters, I shall run the risk of sounding dogmatic by formulating briefly some of my critical assumptions.

I assume the poem itself to be the object of my study, and refer only incidentally to its probable origin in the mind of the poet and to its possible social, moral, and psychological effect upon the reader. My desire is to make an analysis and an evaluation that are literary; therefore, I am concerned with philosophical and moral problems only as they function within the poem to reveal character, create conflict, and intensify dramatic action. I am not dismissing "thought," rather I am using it for literary analysis.

I regard each poem as dramatic, each speaker providing a possible perspective, by no means necessarily Browning's own, from which a philosophical, moral, or aesthetic problem is viewed. In general, I shall not identify the speaker with the poet, but interpret him as a part of the world provided within the poem. The good poem, I assume, furnishes the necessary clues for its explication.

I use the terms *matter, structure*, and *meaning*. By *matter* I mean all the materials out of which the poem is made (sensuous, emotional, and intellectual), and by *structure* all the devices used to arrange and hold matter in artistic form (diction, sentence structure, rhythm, sound repetition, imagery, paradox, irony). Matter is not meaning, nor is it structure. Meaning is that end produced by the union of matter and structure; it is matter completely, satisfyingly expressed, an incarnation in structure.

My purpose is both descriptive and evaluative. I shall make final judgments primarily upon two bases: first, the degree of unity achieved within the work; second, the scope and intensity of the poem—in short, its stimulus to aesthetic responses. I wish also to describe the character and quality of the unity—a tension produced, I shall propose, by a dialectical juxtaposition of opposing material and structural forces—and to suggest the kind and range of aesthetic response which Browning's shorter dramatic poems are likely to produce.

I have no quarrel with those who go outside these limits to discuss Browning's poetry as self-revelation, philosophy, sociology, or history, and I am perfectly aware of the complex forces which unite to produce a finished poem. My present objective, to describe and evaluate the poems themselves, however, can best be achieved through a critical system which, operating within the poem, seeks to make evaluations that are literary.

II

Eve and the Virgin:
Andrea del Sarto

Browning characteristically begins "Andrea del Sarto" in the middle of an action, and concentrates the painter's situation into a single climactic experience. Yet before the drama is finished this pin-pointed moment has been related to the whole of Andrea's drab life. We have both the intense moment of revelation and the slow movement in time of past events which make the painter's final insight possible.

The poem is a psychological study in which the time element is an important part of structure. Andrea's initial surrender to his wife's demand that he paint for money is totally damning to the artist; its completeness and finality divert interest from what may happen to why it has happened, from suspense in action to character analysis. The action moves from present to past, from past to present, and, finally, to an imaginary future in the New Jerusalem. Andrea's restless dissatisfaction with any time signals his personal disturbances, his unwillingness to accept himself in any role, real or imaginary, and provides a significant clue to the poem's meaning.

There can be no question about the sordidness of the present, for Browning presents its most repelling aspects. Andrea, uncomfortable over his capitulation to his wife, seeks renewed self-esteem in the past which he tries to make palatable by recalling what he once was, or what he imagines he was. A less honest nature might have found comfort in such an escape, but Andrea, much too sensitive to be easily deluded, is driven first to face and then to rationalize his obvious failure. Ironically, he achieves not peace, but an increasing self-awareness that makes the past as uncomfortable as the present. In his primitive Garden he finds both the Tree of Knowledge and an Eve. He comes to see that his failure is at least twofold—both as artist and as lover—and that somehow these two are inseparably related. His initial surrender of his art to Lucrezia is paralleled by a final surrender of Lucrezia to her lover. From the reality of both past and present, he is driven finally to seek refuge in an imaginary heaven where, with Leonardo, Rafael, and Agnolo, he achieves illusory fulfillment.

This account of action inadequately describes the drama of the poem, however, for it is given complexity and intensity both by Andrea's conscious attempts to reject what he unconsciously knows to be true, and by a series of dialectical movements within the poem. Part of the intensity comes from the opposition of pairs, all symbolic: summer and autumn, twilight and darkness, youth and age, past and present, heaven and earth, hope and failure.

The first suggestion of meaning comes in the ambivalent subtitle, "The Faultless Painter." The phrase, recognized as ironic, is too often understood to mean that Browning said a thing ridiculous in order to enforce a contradictory meaning. Accordingly, he did not mean that Andrea was faultless, but that he was totally depraved. A thoughtful reading discredits this one-dimensional interpretation. Empson makes a statement about irony which applies here: "An irony has no point unless it is true, in some degree, in both senses; for it is imagined as a part of an argument; what is said is made absurd, but it is what the opponent might say." [1] Precisely so in "Andrea del Sarto." In a sense, Andrea is a faultless painter; at the same time he is a mere craftsman. On another level, he is both husband and pander; Lucrezia is at once his Virgin and his Eve.

Andrea's roles are many and often contradictory. He becomes participant with the lover in a twofold drama, one in which lover and mistress provide contrasting comment upon husband and wife, and the other in which the two vie for Lucrezia's favor. Still again, Andrea is unwittingly cast in opposition to Agnolo and obliged to defend his faultless paintings against his rival's superior accomplishments. Torn between opposite but equally demanding claims and made constantly aware of failure, Andrea achieves not wholeness, but destructive self-realization.

His impulses run in counter directions. A remark of self-justification is followed by one of self-accusation; a spirit of bravado and assertiveness, by one of passive acceptance. His attitude toward Lucrezia fluctuates from contempt to deference; toward the lover, from resentment to grudging admiration; toward his public, from disdain to obsequiousness.

Andrea oscillates between assertiveness and passive-

ness, between projection and receptivity. His vision of
what he should do as artist is remarkably clear and his
desire for a normal relationship with Lucrezia is intense,
but a spiritual and physical enervation prohibits him
from being satisfactorily either the husband or artist.
The conflict of the poem is between asserted artistic and
masculine virility and a steadily increasing awareness of
debility.

Andrea attempts to establish himself by recalling
with justified pride the praise of his contemporaries; he
is, indeed, a facile craftsman, and his attempt to improve
Rafael is not mere bravado. He likes also to fancy himself as being masculine and irresistible. In the lines

> Your soft hand is a woman of itself,
> And mine the man's bared breast she curls inside

the words "bared breast" suggest masculine strength, and
the "soft hand" feminine dependency and affection. The
hand appropriately curls in his, a symbol of the personal
union which he desires.

At the same time, he is aware of the superiority of
Rafael's paintings, and he realizes too that his own sense
of form and line can never compensate for an insight
which he does not have. Simultaneously, he knows that
the lover possesses Lucrezia in a way that he can never
hope to rival. Suspecting that he is incapable of passion
and devoid of masculine attractiveness, Andrea resembles
a character out of the early Auden, Eliot's Prufrock, or
James's Marcher, save that he, perhaps, is more aware of
his deficiency. His despair is produced partly by the
realization that Lucrezia can be, indeed has been, won.
Even as he presses his ineffectual suit, outside waits a

lover to whom she is willingly drawn. His failure and
the lover's success tantalize him into speculation:

> Ah, but what does he,
> The Cousin! what does he to please you more?

If Andrea could answer this question he would at the
same time answer a great many more. For his failure
with Lucrezia is only a part of his total failure as son,
friend, and artist. His strange, almost abnormal devotion
to a woman who has so degraded him cannot have been
other than devastating to his art. Yet, he realizes clearly
that she is not wholly the cause of his failure:

> Beside, incentives come from the soul's self;
> The rest avail not. Why do I need you?
> What wife had Rafael, or has Agnolo?

What he calls lack of incentive from the soul's self
is really passiveness, debility, receptivity. These qualities
make necessary his attempts to escape from time and self
and produce his ultimate weariness and despair.

Stopford Brooke and William Lyon Phelps have
called attention to Andrea's uxoriousness, his "uncon-
querable passion," but have failed to note that what they
speak of is largely illusory. Indeed, Andrea does seem to
give up everything for Lucrezia—his family, his friends,
his integrity, and finally his creative vision; yet with
equal submissiveness he hands her over to the lover at the
end of the poem: "Again the Cousin's whistle! Go, my
Love." His attitude toward her wavers. His subservience
is counterpointed by a bitterness, an antagonism that
makes itself felt much too often to be ignored: "You

don't understand / Nor care . . . ," "Had I been two,
. . ." "Had you enjoined them on me, given me soul,"
"Had you, with these same, but brought a mind!" "And
had you not grown restless. . . ."

Clearly, uxoriousness is only one manifestation of a
more basic weakness. Attracted as he is by Lucrezia's
body, he lacks, nevertheless, the virility of Fra Lippo
Lippi and the passion of Sebald. What seems physical
desire is partly enthusiasm for artistic form, and in the
following it is the craftsman who speaks: "perfect ears
. . . oh, so sweet," "perfect brow, / And perfect eyes,
and more than perfect mouth, / And the low voice.
. . ." Enamoured of his wife's beauty, Andrea runs his
hands through her hair and remarks that it serves to
frame her picture-perfect face:

> Let my hands frame your face in your hair's gold,
> You beautiful Lucrezia that are mine!

Actually, he is surprisingly passive and physically un-
demanding:

> . . . and it seems
> As if—forgive now—should you let me sit
> Here by the window with your hand in mine
> And look a half-hour forth on Fiesole,
> Both of one mind, as married people use,
> Quietly, quietly the evening through,
> I might get up to-morrow to my work
> Cheerful and fresh as ever.

The half-hour over, he states complacently:

> You loved me quite enough, it seems to-night.

That "enough" reflects a characteristic of Andrea's which is given additional emphasis by the poem's structure. Diction, sound repetition, rhythm, and sentence structure all unite to create an impression, emotionally and sensuously, of placidity and greyness, qualities by which Andrea describes his life and work.

The diction, lacking the colorfulness of Fra Lippo Lippi's, is abstract and conceptual rather than perceptive and sensory. There are an unusually large number of substantives and relatively few modifiers, an almost equal number of concrete and abstract nouns. Clear and sharp but not particularly sensuous, the concrete nouns are used primarily to establish character and setting. Many are descriptive or technical: *sun, tree, star, moon, bird, picture, chalk*. Others show a painter's interest in man's anatomy: *hand, head, face, breast, ears, arms, neck, shoulders*. Andrea habitually speaks professionally, detachedly of the human body. It is as model that he refers most often to Lucrezia.

The small number of modifiers suggests subordination of sensuous appeal. Only a few are sensory, and of these, two alone, *grey* and *golden*, appear more than once; even they lose most of their sensuousness since they are used as symbols, as I shall show later. On the whole, the diction in "Andrea del Sarto" contrasts sharply with that of the Ottima-Sebald scene in *Pippa Passes*, where Browning attempts to communicate physicality.

The greater number of modifiers is qualitative and quantitative: *glad, perfect, past, little, same, poor, great, good*, and *better*. Only a sprinkling of adjectives, *sober, pleasant, strange, festal, melancholy*, and *bright*, are romantically atmospheric. Browning begins "Andrea del Sarto" with a simple, straightforward, unemotional statement:

> But do not let us quarrel any more,
> No, my Lucrezia; bear with me for once:
> Sit down and all shall happen as you wish.

Andrea himself suffers from emotional sterility, reflected both by his "faultless" paintings (contrasted with the "soulful" works of his contemporaries) and by his relations with Lucrezia. His pleading, his promises, his bribes, elicit less response from her than the whistle of the lover. Andrea offers everything, the cousin nothing. Yet his "less" is "more," just as Rafael's is.

In "The Bishop Orders His Tomb" Browning partly characterizes the Bishop by frequent repetition of vowel sounds used for purely sensuous effects, but no such attempt is made in "Andrea del Sarto." Governed by the central meaning of the poem, he does avoid cacophony, the general placidity helping to present both in concept and in emotional texture Andrea's "grey world" and his "autumnal" and "twilight" life and work.

There is considerable alliteration, but it does not function primarily to convey sensuousness or to provide poetic decoration. Frequently, it emphasizes idea by calling attention to important thoughts, as in "mine the man's bared breast she curls inside." This line, containing a basic image, commands special attention because of the alliteration. Browning uses repetition (the *l*'s and the *f*'s in the following, for example) to link sentences and to gain conceptual unity and compactness:

  Love, we are in God's hand.
How strange now, looks the life he makes us lead;
So free we seem, so fettered fast we are!
I feel he laid the fetter: let it lie!

My point is that Browning does not use alliteration in
"Andrea del Sarto," as, for example, Swinburne does in
"Dolores," to produce emotional and sensuous effects
apart from meaning. Even when repetition calls attention to lines that appear sensuous the effect is actually
ironic. For example, "Let my hands frame your face in
your hair's gold" counterpoints sensuous with artistic
attraction, passion with a painter's professional appraisal
of a good subject.

  Alliteration is used further as part of rhythm. Stress-
ing lightly conceptually unimportant syllables, and calling attention to others by heavy stress and alliteration,
Browning achieves simultaneously in some lines both the
artistic effect of alliterative verse and an emphasis on
idea. Thus, the rhythmic pattern of the poem becomes a
part of the meaning much more profoundly than by
merely echoing the sense. Though irregular, the poem is
"unmusical" only if judged by Spenserian and Tenny-
sonian standards. Closer to the Wyatt-Donne tradition,
Browning uses a line basically conventional in that it has
a predetermined number of syllables and stresses, but
breaks with the musical tradition in the placement of
syllables within the line, proposing to relate closely what
is felt and said with the manner of saying it, to use
rhythm both to create and to support meaning. The
absence of a strong sensuous movement, such as that, for
example, which creates so vividly the physicality of

Shakespeare's "Venus and Adonis" and Marlowe's "Hero and Leander," emphasizes Andrea's passivity; its brokenness reflects at the same time his psychological chaos.

Andrea's weariness—physical, intellectual, emotional —is expressed both overtly and structurally.

> I often am much wearier than you think,
> This evening more than usual,

he says. And again:

> Too live the life grew, golden and not grey,
> And I'm the weak-eyed bat no sun should tempt
> Out of the grange whose four walls make his world.

Andrea's debility contrasts significantly with Lucrezia's assertiveness.

Such frequently used words as *silver, dream, quietly, evening, grey, greyness, twilight, autumn* create atmosphere and texture more because of their conceptual meaning than their emotional connotations. Their effect, therefore, is clear and sharp rather than vague and diffuse. Browning's diction, here and elsewhere, has a specificity not found in that of any other nineteenth-century poet before Meredith, Hardy, and Hopkins. It was this quality more than any other that recommended him to Ezra Pound in the twentieth century.

The small number of verbs slows down the action and heightens the sense of weariness. Browning uses a minimum of action words:

> I surely then could sometimes leave the ground,
> Put on the glory, Rafael's daily wear,
> In that humane great monarch's golden look,—

One finger in his beard or twisted curl
Over his mouth's good mark that made the smile,
One arm about my shoulder, round my neck,
The jingle of his gold chain in my ear,
I painting proudly with his breath on me,
All his court round him, seeing with his eyes,
Such frank French eyes, and such a fire of souls
Profuse, my hand kept plying by those hearts,—
And, best of all, this, this, this face beyond,
This in the background, waiting on my work,
To crown the issue with a last reward!

In fourteen lines there are only three finite verbs. Others are implied, and participles function suggestively as verbs. By implication and substitution, however, Browning avoids disturbing the quiet autumnal atmosphere with active verbs. Some lines lack even participles:

But all the play, the insight and the stretch—
Out of me, out of me! And wherefore out?

The effect here should be contrasted with that of "Fra Lippo Lippi," where relatively a great many more verbs are used. Obviously, a difference in subject matter requires a difference in technique: Lippo, in contrast to Andrea, is virile and sensuous.

The structure of Andrea's sentences is on one level a projection of his inner emptiness, and on another a suggestion of his struggle against self-realization. They express an unwillingness to grapple realistically with his problem, a passive receptiveness of "fate" that contradicts his half-hearted attempts at assertiveness.

His imperatives, never strong, are characteristically more often entreaties than commands. He timidly requests that Lucrezia grant him partly what by rights he should command wholly. And though numerous, the interrogatory sentences are not at all like Lippo's startling demand:

Come, what am I a beast for?

Andrea's is not a searching mind attempting to discover truth, but a timid one afraid of discovering too much. Lippo, more confident of himself, could with greater comfort face his problems. Andrea's exclamations lack force, the shock of immediate experience and spontaneous utterance having been absorbed by retrospection. The opening sentence reveals an emotional staleness produced by a situation so often repeated that it has lost all immediacy.

Andrea's speech, though not "literary," lacks the colloquial directness, the force, of Lippo's or Bishop Blougram's. Lucrezia is protagonist but not in the sense that Gigadibs and the Watchman are. Symbolic of the whole pattern of Andrea's life, she is in a sense a much richer auditor than either of the others. Her presence in the room, the turn of her head that brings face but not heart, the careless sweep of her skirt against wet paint, her indifference to Andrea's reputation among his contemporaries, her impatience to join her lover all combine to elicit from Andrea a complex response. In a sense, he speaks more to himself than directly to Lucrezia, and although we never forget that she is with him, we feel that she too is overhearing. Actually, the poem belongs somewhere between dramatic conversation and internal monologue. Andrea does not develop his thoughts logically, for he is not reasoning and coming to conclusions;

rather he is reminiscing, justifying, excusing, and accepting. Consequently, units of expression often consist of
conceptual or emotional rather than grammatical groups.
Their unity is imaginative, hence not always immediately
apparent.

These groups are frequently only fragments, many
times containing a series of substantives and few or no
verbs:

> That Francis, that first time,
> And that long festal year at Fontainebleau!

Their fragmentariness, the omission of co-ordinates and
verbs, is significant. The absence of verbs I have already
discussed as one indication of his passiveness. The omission of co-ordinate conjunctions between independent
clauses serves to break the poem into a series of un-
grammatically related reflections, and at the same time
signals his incapacity for integrating counterimpulses
and for forming relationships.

Lack of structural formality creates the impression
of emotional and intellectual instability. In general, Andrea's sentences are of two types: either segmented, brief,
independent clauses frequently not syntactically related
to a larger unit; or complex sentences consisting of introductory independent clauses followed by one or
more subordinate clauses. These complex sentences are
frequently split into two or more segments by interpolations which may or may not be syntactically related:

> Well, I can fancy how he did it all,
> Pouring his soul, with kings and popes to see,
> Reaching, that heaven might so replenish him,

> Above and through his art—for it gives way;
> That arm is wrongly put—and there again—
> A fault to pardon in the drawing's lines,
> Its body, so to speak: its soul is right,
> He means right—that, a child may understand.

The complex sentences, the numerous subordinations, the interpolations, the exclamations, the lack of syntactical connections give the effect of thought in conflict, of intellectual uncertainty and emotional instability. Andrea's aim is self-justification, but since he has not ordered his thinking, he cannot proceed straightforwardly as Lippo does; rather he muses disjointedly and inconclusively on first one aspect and then another of his unpleasant experience. Andrea is afraid to pursue his speculations to a logical conclusion for he partly knows and rejects what he would find if he did.

His sentences reflect the tortured flow of thought that can neither stop nor come to a logical conclusion, a surplus of diffused intensity that decreases the finality of what he says. The *pasticcio* quality of his thinking is demonstrated by the fact that a reader is hardly aware of either the beginning or the end of many of his constructions.

Thus, the dialectical opposition between Andrea's physical and spiritual debility and his effort to avoid self-realization is communicated materially and structurally. These opposing forces are given both more precise definition and artistic unity particularly through symbol. Lucrezia herself is the dominant symbol. Briefly, Andrea's devotion to her "soulless" beauty signifies a personal and artistic deficiency; and her perfidy, fate's compensation to him for his weakness. She is the materialization of his desires for human relationships and artistic achievement, reflecting his erroneous judgment, his false standard of values.

She is the symbol of the emptiness which Andrea comes to understand. He speaks of himself rightly as a "half-man." The famous "Ah, but a man's reach should exceed his grasp" is ironical, for Andrea is vaguely conscious of the discrepancy between his higher vision (personal and artistic) and his spiritual and emotional faculties to achieve; he is tormented by a stimulus greater than his power to respond.

His eventual capitulation and destruction are suggested by a group of frequently repeated words associated with values: *worth, pay, gold, silver, gain, reward*. Each has a literal meaning, but as a group and in context they are also symbolically significant. The two basic adjectives are *golden* and *silver* (grey): in his "kingly days" Andrea enjoyed the monarch's "golden look"; he worked with Francis' arm about him, the jingle of his gold chain in his ears; a "fire of souls" kept his hand plying until "too live the life grew, golden and not grey. . . ." He left the "golden look" of the monarch for the gold of Lucrezia's hair, and his whole world changed:

> . . . the whole seems to fall into a shape
> As if I saw alike my work and self
> And all that I was born to be and do,
> A twilight-piece.

His attitude toward his work changed; seeing it degenerate into a commodity, he came to speak of it in marketplace terms:

> I'll work then for your friend's friend, never fear,
> Treat his own subject after his own way,
> Fix his own time, accept too his own price,
> And shut the money into this small hand
> When next it takes mine.

He uses the same terminology when he attempts to describe the relation between himself and his painting:

> I know both what I want and what might *gain*,
> And yet how *profitless* to know. . . .

The words *gain* and *profitless* suggest the hold which buying and selling have upon him. His painting itself takes on the color of commercialism:

> All is silver-grey
> Placid and perfect with my art.

Lucrezia is blamed because she failed to urge that he "never care for *gain*" (a pun that is ironic). Because of his perverted values, Andrea becomes paradoxical when he recognizes that Rafael, though lacking his technical skill, is the greater painter:

> Yet do much less, so much less, Someone says,
> (I know his name, no matter)—so much less!
> Well, less is more, Lucrezia.

Toward the conclusion of the poem, these market terms appear more frequently and in positions of greater emphasis. Heightening emotion and sharpening the irony, they become effective mediums for expressing meaning. The brick walls appear cemented with fierce bright gold; Andrea took money from Francis; he neglected to give money to his mother and father; he failed to make money for himself and Lucrezia. Most significantly they depict the degeneration of Andrea's standards of values, his genuine confusion, and ultimately his compromise with the tawdry and commonplace. They are all echoed in the lines:

> That Cousin here again? he waits outside?
> Must see you—you, and not with me? Those *loans?*
> More gaming *debts* to *pay?* you smiled for that?
> Well, let smiles *buy* me! have you more to *spend?*
> While hand and eye and something of a heart
> Are left me, work's my *ware,* and what's it *worth?*
> I'll *pay* my fancy.

Here everything is reduced to a mart where the lover makes debts which Andrea must pay, where Lucrezia barters her love, and where Andrea pays for her smiles with second-rate paintings. The climaxing line, "I'll pay my fancy," suggests the ironic state of Andrea's existence: the delight which he finds in his relationship with Lucrezia is capricious, not real, and even for that he pays dearly.

The words *golden* and *grey* have still another meaning. *Grey* best suggests Andrea's passive, colorless personality, and used in contrast to *golden* points up the difference between the life that he now lives and that he once lived; they also suggest, on another level, the breach between his actual existence and his imagined one. There was a time when life itself was golden, but that time is gone: "A common greyness silvers everything. . . ." Dusk falls outside as Andrea talks; dusk has long since settled over his life. Summer has given way to autumn in the natural world; within Andrea's inner world "autumn grows, autumn in everything." The merging of the outer world with the inner illustrates the success with which Browning handles symbol. Andrea's work, as well as his life, has been affected. "All that I was born to be and do" is "a twilight-piece." "My youth, my hope, my art, being all toned down. . . ." This is the figure which he uses to contrast his work with that of his more successful contemporaries. His is the hand of a patient, skilful, but uninspired craftsman, while in the works of his contemporaries "There burns a truer light of God. . . ."

Andrea regrets his lack of light, but at the same time, paradoxically, fears to venture into full day. In one powerful figure he expresses his inner paralysis and brings together the golden-grey with the wall figure. He says, referring to his earlier life with Francis:

> Too live the life grew, golden and not grey,
> And I'm the weak-eyed bat no sun should tempt
> Out of the grange whose four walls make his world.

The emphasis is on the "weak-eyed bat"—the natural lover of darkness. Andrea prefers the calm security and the comforting shades of four walls to the penetrating light of the world. Lucrezia is a symbol of darkness which he welcomes rather than fears, and he follows his own self-destroying impulses when he chooses her in preference to the world of Rafael and Agnolo. Now he lives within his four walls and takes comfort in the dusk of the late afternoon, his only light a false reflection created by a guilty conscience:

> . . . oft at nights
> When I look up from painting, eyes tired out,
> The walls become illumined, brick from brick
> Distinct, instead of mortar, fierce bright gold,
> That gold of his I did cement them with!

His personal limitations are imposed upon his paintings. He realizes that an artist should break through the boundaries of here and now to participate in the limitlessness of eternity. Spiritually and artistically imprisoned, however, he is unable to transcend the market place. His failure sets him apart from his more illustrious contemporaries:

> Their works drop groundward, but themselves, I know,
> Reach many a time a heaven that's shut to me,
> Enter and take their place there sure enough,
> Though they come back and cannot tell the world.
> My works are nearer heaven, but I sit here.

Indeed, it is understandable that in a moment of despair he should say, "I feel he laid the fetter: let it lie!"

Paradoxically, also, he realizes that Lucrezia is a part of his failure and sometimes blames her for the whole of it; yet he holds tenaciously to the small security which she brings. The fact that he legally possesses her beautiful body is comforting compensation for his personal ineffectualness. She is there as a bulwark against complete self-realization.

The epithet "serpentining beauty" is rich in connotations. It calls to mind the Garden of Eden story with its suggestions of feminine deception, loss of innocence, the curse of God, and spiritual death. In a sense, Lucrezia is his Eve; at the same time she is also his Virgin, the prototype of his technically faultless painting. Another expression of his ambivalent attitude toward her appears in the following:

> And the low voice my soul hears, as a bird
> The fowler's pipe, and follows to the snare.

The fowler is a destructive figure; the snare, a kind of trap serving to restrict and imprison. Browning uses the word *snare* and not *trap* because the snare quietly entangles; while a trap, more violent, suggests action inappropriate to the tone of the poem. Here, as in the serpent figure, the emphasis is on deception, and yet it must be noted again that Andrea's is a willing deception. He is the weak-eyed bat who "came home" to Lucrezia. If she were a deceiver, if he were snared, she was also his deliverer; he found a home, a resting place in the snare.

Browning uses these figures to achieve tragic irony. Andrea both desires and fears light, both resents and welcomes the snare; he prefers the grey autumnal shades, yet nostalgically recalls his golden days. His desire to break his prison walls and reach the heaven of others is expressed in the ironic figure coming at the conclusion of the poem:

> What would one have?
> In heaven, perhaps, new chances, one more chance—
> Four great walls in the New Jerusalem,
> Meted on each side by the angel's reed.

Andrea is tragically incapable of either conceiving or enjoying complete freedom.

Actually, in the "bared breast" figure, quoted earlier as an expression of Andrea's desire for a normal marital relationship, the word *bared* is a pun. Literally, it suggests qualities of masculine strength which Andrea desires, at the same time points up the bareness of his soul. There is nothing there for Lucrezia. In fact, ultimately it is Andrea who seeks Lucrezia's breast, not she his. This reversal of roles should be noted. It is Lucrezia who calls, not Andrea; she who is the assertive, Andrea the receptive member of the pair. Andrea's behavior contrasts with that of the lover; his passive submission to Lucrezia's call, with the command of the lover's whistle. Equally ironic and effective as the subtitle is the line: "You beautiful Lucrezia that are mine." For she was never his. It was Andrea's misfortune to know this.

III

Sportive Ladies
and
Patron Saint:
Fra Lippo Lippi

Our first impression of Fra Lippo Lippi is not favorable. Caught in the wrong section of town, obviously tipsy, he attempts with unbecoming jocularity and crudeness to bribe, threaten, and wheedle his way out of an embarrassing situation. Browning begins by inviting us to think the worst of his character and then proceeds with dramatic skill to superimpose meaning upon meaning, forcing us first to modify and finally to reshape our first impression. Initially flippant, Lippo becomes increasingly sober, moves gradually to climactic and complex seriousness, and finally falls into compromise before disappearing into the dawn-dusk. From sensuality to idealism to compromise: this movement within the poem gives "Fra Lippo Lippi" genuine dramatic form and intensity, summarizing at the same time the conflict and contradictions which exist within the monk-painter.

Lippo is caught at the beginning of the poem between the street where "sportive ladies leave their doors ajar" and his monastic lodging. The situation and the terms are symbolic. The street and monastery represent apparently contradictory forces, both religious and artistic, which Lippo is challenged to reconcile. They pose a tension between sensuous beauty and animal passion, on the one hand, and self-abnegation and spiritual discipline on the other; between what on the surface seems artistic naturalism (that it is something more I shall suggest later) and a restricted allegorical symbolism.

Some of Lippo's disturbances, the source of the dramatic conflict, are the same as Andrea's, for he, too, is victim of division and ambivalency. He, however, less subjective than Andrea, externalizes his conflicts so that the dramatic issue becomes an active struggle between conflicting systems of thought and ways of life.

Lippo is obliged to defend himself in an argument which is both an honest attempt toward a spiritual and artistic synthesis and a rationalization for his shortcomings. As protagonist, the watchman is less fully conceived than Lucrezia, and he elicits from Lippo a narrower range of response than she secures from Andrea. Unlike Lucrezia, he fails to embody, to symbolize the whole to which Lippo feels compelled to respond. Consequently, "Fra Lippo Lippi" is, in one sense, less dramatically intense than "Andrea del Sarto."

Yet the poem is, in its own way, dramatic. Lippo is sensitively aware of the street-monastery conflict which finds appropriate expression in situation and action. The poem is never static, but opening with a situation which presents the conflict, it moves steadily toward its dramatic resolution, the description of the "Coronation of the Virgin."

While the action proceeds, the poem is enriched by a series of intersecting dialectical movements. The structure of the poem, the shifts in Lippo's mood and temper, and the backward and forward movement of the argument signal the violent nature of his conflicts. We move from jocularity to seriousness; from sportive ladies to saintly beauty, from artistic integrity to compromise, from moral indignation to complacency, from defiance to deference, from pathos to humor, from emotional effusion to calm logical argument. Particularly effective are the violent transitions from, for example, spring nights and carnival time to the mew and its saints; from light, ribald songs to Saint Jerome knocking at his poor old breast to subdue the flesh.

Lippo is inwardly divided. He is, indeed, sensual. Even he makes no effort to explain away his presence on the street, and one knows that he would be less satisfied than Andrea with hand-holding. There is physicality in his speech. His diction, sharp and clear, displays a firm grasp on the exterior world. Much of his language is earthy and sensuous. His imagery, too, is dominantly concrete.

To see Lippo as merely sensual, however, is to see him partly. Talk of the life force, for example, introduces a series of paradoxes: the street and the Garden, the sportive ladies and the Virgin, animal indulgence and holy reverence. He speaks of the hunger-pinch, meat and drink, and good serge robe as only a part of man's needs.

In spite of his suggestive nudgings and winkings, underneath his blustering he is genuinely embarrassed by the subterfuge which the restrictions of his order induce him to take. Normally sensuous, he rebels against monastic vows:

> You should not take a fellow eight years old
> And make him swear to never kiss the girls.

The pull of life is too strong for him:

> And my whole soul revolves, the cup runs over,
> The world and life's too big to pass for a dream.

Out of this dilemma grows an artistic and moral apology which reacts against the vivid initial impression of Lippo's sensuality. Together they create for dramatic purposes a dialectical tension which reveals Lippo as not merely a sensualist but a thoughtful, though frustrated and often compromising creative artist.

Initially impressed by his worldliness, we are made increasingly aware of his more complex nature by the urgency with which he communicates ideas, by the ideas themselves, and by the structure of the poem: diction, sentence structure, and imagery.

After the first few moments, after the back-slapping and bribing, Lippo's mood changes and he argues in earnest. Caught in an embarrassing situation, he is forced to develop his defense on the spot. His argument, therefore, is not formal and fixed as that in "Saul" seems to be, but alive, developing, dramatic. Its structural wholeness results from Lippo's intellectual and emotional stability and his eagerness to communicate, characteristics everywhere apparent.

The diction is heavily substantival-verbal, a fact

which, although not arbitrarily emphasizing concept, provides a medium more expressive of idea than of sensuousness. Its precision, reflecting accurate observation and clear thinking, should be contrasted with the vague emotional suggestiveness of Shelley's or Tennyson's language. Browning's care in his choice of words reminds one of Donne or Pound. Indeed, what Pound said of Donne might also be said of Browning: "In Donne's best work we 'find again' a real author saying something he means and not simply 'hunting for sentiments that will fit his vocabulary.'" [1] The relatively few modifiers, primarily qualitative and quantitative, contribute to the conceptual emphasis of the poem, challenging the judgment and inviting evaluation: *poor, great, old, little, fine, good, better*.

Both the frequency and quality of the verbs convey Lippo's compelling desire to reach his listener. Mainly active, they are characterized by strength and movement. Many contain explosive consonants: *snap, whipped, bite, peep, splashed, prodded,* and *clap*. Others are guttural: *shake, funked, gag, stick,* and *suck*. A great many express action phonetically: *twinkle, snap, munching, fling, splashed, prodded, scuttle, clap*. In addition to appearing a natural expression of Lippo's own personality, these words are suited for conversation addressed to the watchman.

Repetition and rhythm, devices which might readily convey sensuousness, function importantly to stress idea. Alliteration serves a number of ends. In the following lines, alliteration of key words points up important meanings, at the same time subordinates others:

Scarce had they turned the corner when a titter
Like the skipping of rabbits by moonlight,—three
    slim shapes,
And a face that looked up . . . zooks, sir, flesh
    and blood,
That's all I'm made of! Into shreds it went,
Curtain and counterpane and coverlet,
All the bed-furniture—a dozen knots,
There was a ladder! Down I let myself,
Hands and feet, scrambling somehow, and so dropped,
And after them. I came up with the fun
Hard by Saint Laurence, hail fellow, well met.

The forward pull of the alliteration, the emphasis on key words, the recurring sounds, the numerous explosives and dentals, and the hard gutturals give the whole a staccato rhythm that carries the reader almost without pause through the entire passage. Alliteration serves the dual purpose of achieving conversational cadence and of emphasizing thought. Often alliteration heightens satiric meaning, as for example:

Their betters took their turn to see and say.
Mazed, motionless and moonstruck—I'm the man!

In such passages as the following, conversational units broken at the end of lines are often held together by alliteration:

From good old gossips waiting to confess
Their cribs of barrel-droppings, candle-ends,—
To the breathless fellow at the altar-foot,
Fresh from his murder.

Alliteration serves also as one means of portraying character. The recurring *m*'s in the following lines, for example, produce conversational unity and cadence, suggesting at the same time the monk's mincing piety and empty formalism:

> Six words there,
> While I stood munching my first bread that month:
> "So, boy, you're minded," quoth the good fat father
> Wiping his own mouth, 'twas refection-time,—
> "To quit this very miserable world?
> "Will you renounce" . . . "The mouthful of bread?"
> thought I;
> By no means! Brief, they made a monk of me.

In that part of the passage belonging to the narrator, Lippo's contrasting disrespect for traditional expression is subtly conveyed by his satiric echoing of the *m* sound; and the phrase "good fat father," deprecatorily suggestive, reflects his temperamental separation from his superiors. Further, throughout the poem his innate distaste for their piousness is conveyed partly through grotesque or unusual words, often given prominence by alliteration, for example, "Fag on at flesh."

The metrical structure and the movement of line, too, are ideally suited for colloquy and argument. Varying in length from nine to thirteen syllables, the line sometimes has more, sometimes less than five stresses, placement of which is not determined by the conventional foot. The line rather consists of a series of time-sense units composed of any number of syllables of which either one may be stressed or of which two or more may share the stress.

Sentence structure is closely correlated with meaning: it reflects sensitively the dramatic situation, changing in form and tone as Lippo moves from one stage of his drama to the next. Initially explosive, the sentences reflect Lippo's immediate surprise at being caught and also the intensity of feeling which he has long curbed but which now at last, under the influence of wine and with rational excuse, he releases. They contrast with the more sustained, more deliberate statements of the middle and latter sections of the poem. Their fragmentariness suggests Lippo's lack of inhibition, the intensity of thought and feeling that throbs in his head and presses for expression. Though always coherent, the sentences in the earlier part are less consciously formulated than those in which he later tries to express his theory of art, or, still later, those in which he rationalizes his failure. The early part of the poem is constantly interrupted by interspersed bits of song, the last of these appearing two-thirds of the way through the poem. Their obvious sensuality and their suggestiveness represent one side of Lippo's character and supply by implication information not directly given in the poem. In contrast to the other sentences, they are initially not only more frequent but more sustained, more lengthy. As Lippo becomes increasingly sober, subduing his sensuality, they appear less often and in more fragmentary form. Further, they suggest Lippo's changing attitude. The first and the last refer to death, but with entirely different implications and in a way which, when the two are placed in juxtaposition, becomes especially meaningful:

> Flower o' the broom,
> Take away love, and our earth is a tomb!

makes life and love synonymous, death a thing which can be ignored or indefinitely postponed. The last, "Death for us all, and our own life for each," counterpoints against the thoughtless hedonism a sense of life's deeper meaning, even of man's responsibility.

When we expand our discussion to include analysis of the formal elements of sentence structure, we note first that cadence is one of the most important. Browning, attempting to reproduce a conversational rhythm, sought his pattern in the speaking voice. Other poets of the eighteenth and nineteenth centuries wrote dramatic poetry; some of them wrote dramatic monologues, but none came so near as Browning to reproducing prose rhythms. This is not to say, of course, that none could have, or that Browning is "better" because he did. It does suggest, however, one characteristic important both for its meaning in Browning's poetry, and for its influence upon twentieth-century poets, particularly upon Pound, who in a significant way adopted Browning's mode of speaking.

The effect of cadence upon tone, texture, and meaning in "Fra Lippo Lippi" is apparent especially in the following:

> Aha, you know your betters! Then, you'll take
> Your hand away that's fiddling on my throat,
> And please to know me likewise. Who am I?
> Why, one, sir, who is lodging with a friend
> Three streets off—he's a certain . . . how d'ye call?
> Master—a . . . Cosimo of the Medici,
> I' the house that caps the corner. Boh! you were best!

Here Browning's faithfulness to the actual movement of the speaking voice shapes a medium in which matter is enhanced by structure. The impulsive, fragmentary character of the sentences precisely reflects Lippo's initial mood.

A few of the sentences are long, containing asyntactical elements and presenting a series of conceptual or emotional rather than grammatical and logical units. None, however, is imaginatively or intellectually chaotic. In the following, for example, there is no real confusion:

> But, mind you, when a boy starves in the streets
> Eight years together, as my fortune was,
> Watching folk's faces to know who will fling
> The bit of half-stripped grape-bunch he desires,
> And who will curse or kick him for his pains,—
> Which gentleman processional and fine,
> Holding a candle to the Sacrament,
> Will wink and let him lift a plate and catch
> The droppings of the wax to sell again,
> Or holla for the Eight and have him whipped,—
> How say I?—nay, which dog bites, which lets drop
> His bone from the heap of offal in the street,—
> Why, soul and sense of him grow sharp alike,
> He learns the look of things, and none the less
> For admonition from the hunger-pinch.

This sentence is spoken by a mind so pregnant with ideas that subordination follows subordination, every thought suggesting an elaboration, an explanation, an example. Firm intellectual and emotional control shapes what might have been chaotic into an organized, coherent expression. Although lacking syntactical unity, it has emotional and intellectual unity. Conversationally it is right. Lippo has begun at this point in the poem his self-defense, and the increasing seriousness implied both in the content and structure of this sentence should be contrasted with the irresponsible jocularity suggested by the structure of the passage quoted in the preceding paragraph.

Most of the sentences, however, are very short—many no more than one or two lines in length; others are only word groups suggesting conceptual or emotional reactions. Those in the earlier part of the poem appear a great deal shorter because they are more telegraphic and are less closely related to each other by transitional thoughts and language. These short sentences communicate Lippo's mental alertness. He does not fumble with his thoughts, play with his ideas, wander hopelessly because he is unable or fears to arrive at a conclusion. He speaks straightforwardly, confidently. In the first part of the poem he is compelled by physical excitement; in the second, by enthusiasm for idea; only toward the end does he hesitate:

> —That is—you'll not mistake an idle word
> Spoke in a huff by a poor monk, God wot,
> Tasting the air this spicy night which turns
> The unaccustomed head like Chianti wine!
> Oh, the church knows! don't misreport me, now!

At this point the structural tension relaxes for a moment to reflect Lippo's temporary uncertainty and to prepare the reader for the climactic description of the "Coronation of the Virgin." Throughout, one hears the speaking voice—bullying, reasoning, cajoling. The rising or falling inflections, the change in pitch, and the pause suggest Lippo's attitude and help convey his meaning.

His speech is colloquial also in that it contains no

words ordinarily omitted in conversation. There is no padding for rhetorical effect or for the sake of conventional meter. The omissions, however, are of a different kind than those in "Andrea del Sarto." Andrea's talk, much of it directed to himself, has some of the aspects of internal monologue. Important elements of the sentence—even the subject and verb—are frequently omitted. The poem gives the impression of half-formed thoughts and blurred emotional and sensuous impressions. Fra Lippo, on the other hand, talking directly to someone, presents his case with directness and conviction. His purpose is clear, sharp communication of ideas. His omissions, rarely nouns and verbs, help maintain the syntax and cadence of conversation: the ordinary shortening of verbs, some ellipses, a few articles, and an occasional preposition.

The many declarative sentences give the poem positiveness. The numerous exclamatory sentences suggest immediacy of emotional and sensuous reaction, giving strength to Lippo's personality and color and force to his speech. The questions, some of them rhetorical, are structural devices which isolate and emphasize important issues, providing Lippo opportunity to express his own ideas.

His increasing sobriety, his obviously sincere argument, and a mass of structural devices gradually rectify the initial impression that Lippo is a sensualist. As the poem develops, he emerges as a complex, sometimes contradictory, person, capable of being understood only in terms of his response to the equally demanding, equally attractive pull of his two worlds, the monastery and the street.

So organic are these cross-purpose forces that they become part of the structure. Lippo speaks a polyglot language picked up primarily from both the streets and monastery. The juxtaposition of these alien jargons appears grotesque and amusing on the surface, but in actuality provides an important clue to understanding the poem. His street diction is earthy and sensuous; his monastery diction is abstract and intellectual. Lippo himself is both.

To refine a little, his diction operates on two levels: the learned and the colloquial, representing the humanistic-monastic dichotomy. The learned words include such Latin derivatives as *munificent, subtle, miserable, renounce, admonition, leisure, passion, triumph, homage,* and *instigate.* On the colloquial level he uses one syllable words such as *zooks, take you, mum, wink, crib, funked, gag, huff, hip* to *haunch.* Additionally present, such "poetic" words as *eve, hap, wot, ere, quoth, harbours, o'er, bethought, betwixt, marge, a-dangle, a-making,* and *a-painting* seem not intended to create romantic remoteness. In spite of their "literary" quality, most of them are easily adapted to colloquial cadence; some of them are used humorously to point up grotesqueness ("quoth the good fat father"). They combine with the learned and conversational to show the diverse influences which Lippo has absorbed into his grotesque personality; they suggest his cosmopolitanism and habit of synthesizing.

One of the most effective expressions of conflict is in the rhythm. The poem is basically, though with many deviations, iambic pentameter. Many of the lines have only four stresses literally, however, or only four functionally, since one is greatly subdued. This creates an effect reminiscent of alliterative verse in which Browning had a continuing interest. A competent musician, he found shifting time no more inconsistent in poetry than in music and alternated between the four and five beat lines, or, more importantly, superimposed one upon the other, expressing through the counterpoint a major theme of the poem. For example:

> Her *pair* of *ear*rings and a *bunch* of *flow*ers.
> Of the mu*ni*ficent *House* that *har*bours *me*.
> A *wood-coal* or the *like?* or *you* should *see!*
> To *roam* the *town* and *sing* out *car*nival.
> *Mum*'s the *word* *nat*urally; but a *monk*!
> And so a*long* the *wall*, *o*ver the *bridge*.

A sensitive ear hears two metrical patterns and is aware of both dissonance and harmony; or, at best, dissonance being absorbed into harmony.

Rhythm, then, expresses the conflict, indeed, goes beyond that to suggest a concurrently operating, equally strong, synthesizing force. Both diversity and reconciliation are seen also in the imagery. Many images undergo a transformation converting what appears abstract into sensuous, or conversely, sensuous into abstract. For example, Lippo asks, "Can't I take breath and try to add life's flash . . . ?" *Life's flash* is basically abstract, but the use of the sensuous *flash* for something immaterial and the juxtaposition of the two words make it other than abstract in its effect. Life which the prior tried to explain apart from materiality becomes both immaterial and material to Lippo, and in his imagination is associated with fire.

There is an ironic inversion of values in the one well-known metaphor which Lippo borrows from the Old Testament. "And my whole soul revolves, the cup runs over," he says, referring to physical rather than spiritual fullness. Aware of antagonisms between street and monastery, Lippo searches for a unifying principle. He is not intellectually timid or merely confused; he does not occupy middle ground for lack of convictions; he is not an opportunist shifting positions as self-interest dictates. At his best, he thinks honestly, clearly, creatively, synthetically, and in the blurring of division lines he points toward reconciliation of two areas of experience considered irreconcilable by his peers.

Lippo's purpose is integration, and for such a task he is naturally endowed. In contrast to Andrea's emptiness he is fully alive, intellectually, emotionally, and sensuously. Two passages, from many possible ones, illustrate his method of thinking. Both pose questions illustrative of his intellectual honesty and his desire to arrive at truth:

> Though your eye twinkles still, you shake your head—
> Mine's shaved—a monk, you say—the sting's in that!
> If Master Cosimo announced himself,
> Mum's the word naturally; but a monk!
> Come, what am I a beast for? tell us, now!
>
> What would men have? Do they like grass or no—
> May they or mayn't they? all I want's the thing
> Settled for ever one way.

Discarding conventional thinking, he introduces moral issues of revolutionary possibilities. He delights in juxtaposing conflicting worlds of thought in order to achieve the more nearly adequate synthesis toward which he aspires.

Influenced by his environment, he formulates ideas from recalcitrant materials. His early life on the streets gives him insight beyond that of the ordinary monk; and perhaps for this reason his experience within the order has left upon him a less traditional, more personal imprint. A grotesque mixture of monk and man, he is peculiarly fitted for the task of reconciliation. He has retained his close contact with the world, and his awareness of spiritual values—in spite of his little respect for monasticism. His problem is to achieve integration in his painting, to bring together successfully body and soul, nature and spirit.

Perhaps his most distinguishing characteristic is his creativity. It marks his thought both as artist and moralist. His natively creative mind finds outlet particularly in his use of words. Frequent ungrammatical formations and constructions show his disregard for convention and his willingness to experiment. Word creations and compounds suggest his inventiveness. His compoundings, in various forms, demonstrate particularly his intellectual vitality and ingenuity; they are products of a synthesizing mind.

His individuality and creativeness show also in his use of numerous words and expressions which are found nowhere else in Browning's poetry. For the most part, these words emphasize important aspects of Lippo's personality—his mental alertness, his creativeness, his catholicity—or they serve to place him more realistically in his milieu. Among the most suggestive are *disemburdening*, *fag, fooleries, phiz, spicy, misreport, bowery, kirtle, funked, harry, weke, fiddling, zooks, ouf, stinger, straw-fire, devil's-game, angel-brood, gullet's gripe.* The number of these words (forty in all) indicates the care Browning took to make Lippo an individual, and at the same time serves as a warning against too facile generalizations about Browning's diction.

Lippo uses his capacities to achieve, partly, the reconciliation which he seeks. He asserts that all of life is good and that each part of it can lead to a fuller realization of God. He accepts it all—flesh and spirit—and in protest against the monastic dichotomy insists that man achieves his highest development through a process of inclusion and synthesis which dedicates both body and soul to the best of which they are capable.

His artistic concepts develop naturally from this interpretation of life. Nature reveals God when it is interpreted and ordered by a creative mind:

> Art was given for that;
> God uses us to help each other so,
> Lending our minds out.

Thus, the artist converts nature into humanly significant forms, discovering God in the process. His purpose is to illuminate the mind, to order the emotions, to sharpen the senses. He treats not a philosophy, a code, a dogma, but a set of values, relationships, meanings:

> For, don't you mark? we're made so that we love
> First when we see them painted, things we have passed
> Perhaps a hundred times nor cared to see;
> And so they are better, painted—better to us,
> Which is the same thing.

The end of art is understanding and sympathy, not action:

> Why, for this
> What need of art at all? A skull and bones,
> Two bits of stick nailed crosswise, or, what's best,
> A bell to chime the hour with, does as well.

The issue clarifies when we contrast what Lippo defends with what he attacks. He protests against one-dimensional symbolism, abstract appeals for morality, allegorical representations such as those which cover the walls of medieval churches. Ecclesiastical art of the Middle Ages, often beautiful in conception and execution, was far removed from flesh-and-blood reality; its avowed purpose was to teach, to call upon men to separate themselves from a sinful world. Embracing the whole of God's creation as good (the town's fair face, the river's line, the mountain round, the figures of man, woman, and child) Lippo uses art to teach a love for the world that would seem blasphemous to a medieval theologian. His apparent espousal of realism or even naturalism in art, however, is deceptive. "I'm a beast, I know," he remarks ironically, and straightforwardly he contradicts himself. Actually, he does not discard symbolism but discovers a new source of symbols. The world, instead of being a snare, becomes to him a declaration of God's glory, and his purpose is to show that glory by painting common, ordinary things in an honest, realistic manner. To Lippo a proper appreciation of Nature is sacramental in a way that contradicts a great deal of medieval teaching. Actually, his basic quarrel with the monastery is theological even though he discusses it in artistic terms.

From the nobility of his conception, however, he lapses at the end of the poem into a reality less lofty. We are checked at the point of persuasion by Lippo himself. After all, to what extent is his argument a rationalization?

> It's natural a poor monk out of bounds
> Should have his apt word to excuse himself.

As penance for his night out he pledges himself to paint a picture, a description of which brings us once more to recognize his paradox. His motives are mixed: it is conceived as a peace offering, yet, in contemplation of it his imagination kindles and he is swept far beyond his initial objectives. Jocularity gives way to earnestness as he visions a host of pious, pure saints, into whose company he, though unworthy, is drawn. They are attending, significantly, the coronation of the Virgin. The painting becomes a kind of penitential office through which Lippo is cleansed (his particular sin is that he has reduced woman to a mere animal) and made a part of the holy communion. "A sweet angelic slip of a thing [his divine mistress] . . . puts out a soft palm" and leads him into the "celestial presence." But clay that he is, Lippo cannot long abide the rarified atmosphere. The spread of wings is transformed into a kirtle under which he, until disturbed by the hothead husband, plays hot cockles with the angelic form now become something less.

This picture is a symbol of Lippo's whole experience. Perhaps he lacks the necessary moral strength and courage to effect a more nearly perfect integration than this last effort achieves. Perhaps the end which he envisions is too difficult for any man. His final artistic compromise, his last roguish remarks before disappearing into the morning light (and back to the darkness of his mew) bring our minds back once more to the beginning of the poem. And we know that there will be more paintings which serve as peace offerings to his order, more night escapades, and more internal struggle and intellectual searching. In "Andrea del Sarto" the deepening dusk symbolizes Andrea's artistic and moral deterioration; in "Fra Lippo Lippi" also light is symbolic. The poem begins in darkness with the face of Lippo only dimly lighted by the watchman's torch; but as the painter gropes his way toward a clearer understanding of himself and his mission, the morning dawns murkily, its dimness a symbol of Lippo's partly successful, partly unsuccessful attempt to integrate monastery and street into one clear vision.

IV

*Ecclesiastical Vision
in Stone:
The Bishop
Orders His Tomb*

The first clue to the meaning of "The Bishop Orders His Tomb" is given in the title. Browning originally called the poem "The Tomb at St. Praxed's," but neither that nor "The Bishop" appears to have pleased him. In the final version he linked the two and inserted the word *orders*. In what sense does the Bishop "order" his tomb? The apparent discrepancy between what he requests and what he gets proposes that the title is ironic and suggests an approach to the poem's meaning. The critic's task is largely one of pursuing this suggestion.

The irony of the poem arises from the juxtaposition of two ways of seeing and two standards of values. "The Bishop Orders His Tomb" is not a persuasive for any point of view or code of behavior, that is, the discrepancies do not exist between Browning's obviously "right" world and the Bishop's obviously "wrong" one. In this respect it is different from "A Modest Proposal," in which Swift establishes the conflict as existing between himself and a somewhat indefinite opposition. We are always conscious of the writer's presence and feel the force of his moral indignation.

In "The Bishop Orders His Tomb," as in "Andrea del Sarto" and "Fra Lippo Lippi," Browning's personality has been, to quote Joyce, "refined out of existence," and the poem is permitted to speak for itself. The result is objective drama rather than subjective didacticism. The discrepancies which produce the irony, then, must exist within the poem itself. They are provided primarily by diverse ways of seeing the Bishop and his world. First, there is the view arising from the facts of the poem; then, there is the narrower, more subjective one of the Bishop himself. That these two views are not correlative is immediately apparent. In "Andrea del Sarto," the conflicting forces exist within the character, making the poem psychological and tragic; here, although the Bishop is not entirely without inner struggle, the major discrepancy occurs between his view of himself and the external reality. Of all the characters included in this study, the Bishop of St. Praxed's is the only one not known definitely to refer to an historical personage and not to be given a name. It is the only poem the title of which directs attention more to an action than to a character; in fact, in the original title the name of the character did not appear at all.

Browning's task was to write the poem so that the two points of view would be precisely communicated in an effective, compelling manner. The representation of the Bishop and his objective world was the easier task, accomplished by a selection of significant incident, a use of full, rich details and precise language. To convey the Bishop's subjective view of himself was more difficult. The Bishop was confused, a fact dramatically revealed by the variance between his fully conscious and his semi-conscious speech. In the former, we see the Bishop as he habitually thought of himself and as he faced the world—"popes, cardinals, and priests." In the latter, we penetrate a region strange even to the Bishop and glimpse there the half-formed thoughts, imprecise emotions, and moral confusion. Browning intended the Bishop's incoherent speech to be an interpretive comment upon his inner confusion, as he suggests: "In St. Praxed, the blunder as to the sermon is the result of the dying man's haziness; he would not reveal himself as he does but for that." [1] Communication of this subconscious level of meaning requires a technique which the poet had been developing since *Sordello*. I shall say more about it later.

It is easy to underestimate the fullness and complexity of Browning's treatment of the Bishop. As a character, he lives in a smaller world and is less complexly motivated than either Fra Lippo Lippi or Andrea del Sarto, lacking the intellectual vigor and the moral concern of the one, and the inner conflicts of the other. In this respect he is more like Jonson's characters than Shakespeare's. However, his presentation in the poem is complete and satisfying. Eliot distinguishes between the "surface qualities" of Beaumont and Fletcher's work and Ben Jonson's by saying that the formers' is superficial with a vacuum behind it, but that Jonson's superficies are solid.[2] So with Browning's Bishop. His world is limited, but it is fully conceived and convincingly communicated; intellectually and emotionally the Bishop is a logical part of it. He escapes being burlesque, as do many of Jonson's characters, because in relation to his world he is not incongruous. The superficialities, we recognize, are in the Bishop as man, not in the poem.

Pride is a distinguishing characteristic of the Bishop, and an important ironic tension arises from the disparity between his imagined and his obviously real status. The most frequently repeated words in his vocabulary are *I* and *mine*. His sense of exaggerated self-importance isolates him from other people, whom he fails to distinguish from things. Either they are objects to use or barriers to overcome. "A Jew's head cut off at the nape" is simply a thing to designate the size of a piece of lapis lazuli. He speaks of God as a statue and of himself in his immortal state as a piece of sculpture. The mother and the sons have "eyes as a lizard's quick." Conversely, he gives life to the inanimate: "a sunbeam's sure to lurk," "impoverished frieze," "starved design."

Isolated by his pride, the Bishop feels no great need for human relationships. Andrea, enamoured of Lucrezia, betrays friend and parent; yet he experiences always a real desire for companionship, and his personal failure with people is one of the tragedies of his life. The Bishop, incapable of such tragedy, is, on the other hand, a mere collector. The sons' mother was a major acquisition along with his villas, baths, manuscripts, and art objects. She, of course, was forbidden him by the laws of his church, and the sons were illegitimate; but neither she nor they created for him a moral problem. He regretted only that she was greedy, a charge that has at least two implications. In context, the Bishop seems ironically to accuse her of loving material things. More obviously, having loved and got her body, he rationalizes that she tried to get his soul, a word which itself is ambiguous. At the conclusion of the poem his single comfort is that he won her, not because he loved her but because she was fair and Gandolf envied him.

He shows the same insensitiveness toward his sons. They are pleasant reminders of his triumph over Gandolf, and he hopes to use them to achieve his last great desire. Significantly, I think, with one exception they remain unnamed, impersonal. Their unresponsiveness to their father's request must reflect his long disinterest in them. The lines, "Nay, boys, ye love me . . ." and "Sons, all have I bequeathed you . . ." are ironic. The Bishop has felt no need for companionship, and his contempt for people makes his dependence upon the sons at the conclusion of the poem especially meaningful. His appeal to Anselm suggests his desperation, and the son's unfeeling rebuff indicates how little he had cultivated human relationships.

His frustration is not so tragic as Andrea's. In fact, there is an undercurrent of sardonic humor in "The Bishop Orders His Tomb," a characteristic which became increasingly important in Browning's poetry as he matured. The Bishop's hatred for Gandolf, obviously a threat to his pre-eminence, is so intense that at times it becomes ludicrous. His grotesque pride, objectified in the elaborate tomb, contrasts sharply with the futility of the opening line of the poem, "Vanity, saith the preacher, vanity!" the meaning of which the Bishop only vaguely apprehends.

His preoccupation in this life has been cultural, materialistic, and sensuous; and his achievements may be viewed from either his own perspective or from the more objective one provided by the whole poem. Eventually, of course, they must be viewed from both, for the poem's meaning lies in the tension created by these disparate views. The Bishop's distorted sense of values, intensely acquisitive spirit, and inflexible will provide another paradoxical contrast both to the first line of the poem and to the situation at the conclusion.

The Bishop is a man of external brilliance, displaying catholic learning in his allusions to ancient literature and art, in his cultivated speech, and in his vocabulary, which is learned rather than colloquial. Characteristically, he uses such words as *limb*, *carrion*, and *conflagration*, sharp contrasts to Lippo's more homely diction. He has a wide range of artistic interests, admiring the mosaics of angels (and incidentally the sunbeams), the paintings, the statuary in the church, a good line of poetry, the beauty of the ritual. A learned vocabulary, formal tone, rhetorical elegance, balanced and periodic sentences, and Latin syntax give polish and elegance to his speech. All in all, he would have found the suave Duke of "My Last Duchess" socially acceptable.

Appropriately, there are more decorative elements in "The Bishop Orders His Tomb" than in either "Fra Lippo Lippi" or "Andrea del Sarto." Moreover, they are used in a different manner. In the latter two poems there exists between them and the prose meaning of the line a closer relationship. They are intended to clarify and heighten total meaning. In "The Bishop Orders His Tomb" the relation is more remote and they are used symbolically rather than presentationally. They communicate the Bishop's surface brilliance, yet at the same time betray an inflexible and uncreative mind. His vision of himself in marble is suggestive: he is a finely shaped, basically inanimate product of his culture. And the Bishop is proud of this.

Among the more obvious decorative devices are rhetorical balance, sound repetition, and a pronounced, regular rhythm. It is important to note that all these are contrapuntal, not harmonic, with the thought of the line. Except in his moments of incoherency, the Bishop uses phrasal and sentence balance and parallelism, sometimes reinforcing these devices with alliteration:

> Big as a Jew's head cut off at the nape,
> Blue as a vein o'er the Madonna's breast.

He frequently uses words in pairs, not to intensify thought by repetition, but to create sensuously pleasing cadence: "tooth and nail . . . ," "the rare, the ripe," "rosy and flawless," "see and burst."

Similarly, repetition of words, consonants, and vowels appeals more to the ear than to the mind. There is more alliteration than usual, sometimes several letters carrying through a number of lines to form intense emotional and sensuous groups. In addition to repeating vowels and consonants within the line, Browning repeats them also at the end so that they function as rhyme might, for example: *missed—dig, beneath—me, south—same, line—lurk, peach—prize, well—once—was*. The effect, though more subtle than rhyme, is perceptible.

Rhythmically, "The Bishop Orders His Tomb" is one of the most nearly regular of Browning's dramatic monologues. Every line has ten syllables, and for the most part the stress pattern, though not strictly iambic, is basically regular.

The total effect of the Bishop's rhetorical and sententious style suggests a superficiality of which the divorce of structural devices from thought is symbolic. The sterility of his mind is suggested by his formal sentence structure. He is more fixed than Andrea and less creative than Lippo. Andrea does not suffer from intellectual rigor mortis even if he is incapable of action; Lippo's fertile mind can be expressed only in an erratic and heavily subordinate sentence structure. The Bishop's more limited sphere is communicated appropriately in a stylized and rigid structure. In his normal state, he has neither the emotional nor intellectual impulse to break through the bounds established by rhetorical discipline. It is only when he faces death and frustration that his sentence structure breaks down—of this I shall speak later. His typical sentence is the co-ordinate consisting of two or more unmodified independent clauses with or without a correlative:

Draw round my bed: is Anselm keeping back?

                         I fought
With tooth and nail to save my niche, ye know:
—Old Gandolf cozened me, despite my care;
Shrewd was that snatch from out the corner South
He graced his carrion with, God curse the same!

He also uses the periodic sentence, a construction equally as formal and, in the Bishop's hands, as inflexible. He attempts two long periodics, neither of which he completes for reasons which I shall offer in another connection.

His lack of ingenuity and his subservience to established pattern are further suggested by his Latinisms: his use of the absolute construction; his placement of object before verb, modifier after substantive, and verb at the end of the clause.

The decorative elements of his style, then, perform a double function. They mark him a man of learning and culture, but at the same time, because of their tenuous relationship to the thought of the poem, suggest his lack of intellectual and moral depth. Understanding this enables us to view the Bishop from two perspectives.

Both his materialism and his sensuousness are reflected in his diction. Most of his nouns are concrete. Among the few abstract ones, those which occur most frequently, *God, death, life, peace,* and *world,* are habitually converted into materialistic values. The word *God* appears seven times, five of which are in the form of an exclamation: "ah, God!" "God curse the same!" "God, ye wish it!" He thinks of the Deity as an anthropomorphic being: once by referring to Him as a marble statue, and again by emphasizing the purely physical aspect of the mass. The mass, the candle flames, the incense smoke are all conceived on a sensuous, materialistic level. Eternity is actually an extension of time in which life is continued on a worldly plane—the only apparent difference being the greater advantages it provides the Bishop. One moment he contemplates projection of his political maneuvering on a wider scale, only to be reminded the next of the embarrassment of being humiliated before old Gandolf. He thinks of himself in eternity as a statue which still possesses the sensibilities and passions of a man. His single use of the word *soul*,

> Ever your eyes were as a lizard's quick,
> They glitter like your mother's for my soul,

indicates by the lines which follow that it has some very close relation to his possessions. He uses abstract words, then, as part of the traditional vocabulary of a Bishop, but constantly transmutes them from spiritual to material signs. Even the words which often are used abstractly remain concrete: *church* designates a specific building and *pulpit*, a platform in that building.

There are more adjectives, dominantly sensuous, in this poem than in "Andrea del Sarto," "Fra Lippo Lippi," or "Bishop Blougram's Apology." Every sense is addressed, but the poem appeals particularly to sight, touch, and smell. It contains some of the most sensuous lines in Browning:

> As fresh-poured red wine of a mighty pulse.
> And mistresses with great smooth marbly limbs.

The sensuous immediacy of these lines is strengthened by a deft manipulation of movement. In the verse "And mistresses with great smooth marbly limbs" the voice is held by the long vowels to linger sensuously over each word so that a basic part of the meaning is conveyed structurally. "Good strong thick stupefying incense-smoke" illustrates another technique. The long vowels slow the speed of the line, and the flanking consonants bring the voice almost to a stop between each word. The line is doubly slowed to give it the requisite ponderousness. "I fought / With tooth and nail to save my niche" is given rapid staccato tempo by the dominance of consonants.

It is important to note that Browning's use of adjectives is not merely presentational. There are no passages in "The Bishop Orders His Tomb" that equal the visual brilliance of Keats's "The Eve of St. Agnes." Browning aims at something different—a response that is psychological as well as sensuous. We must exempt this poem from Eliot's charge that Browning and Tennyson "do not feel their thoughts as immediately as the odour of a rose." [3] Here Browning does what Eliot says a poet must: in addition to the heart he looks also "into the cerebral cortex, the nervous system, and the digestive tracts." The result is a union of thought and sensation. Browning exploits that level of experience on which thought, sense, and emotion cease to be dissociated entities and merge into one pattern. The result is such expressions as "to revel down," "impoverished frieze," "starved design," "marbly limbs," "brave Frascati villas," which express a complex experience that must be perceived psychically and physically by the entire nervous and muscular system.

Even the Bishop's qualitative adjectives are sensuous, few of them implying absolute values. He prefers, for example, *great* and *strong* to *good*, and uses *evil* merely to suggest unpleasantness. His quantitative adjectives and most of his adverbs have to do primarily with time and space. He speaks only of the now, of specific units of measurement, and of the future as hours, days, centuries.

He is attracted particularly by the sensuous qualities

of both art and religion: the blue vein over the Madonna's breast, the brilliant colorings, the tactile qualities in all forms of art, and the hearing, seeing, feeling, tasting appeal of the ritual:

> And *hear* the blessed mutter of the mass,
> And *see* God made and eaten all day long,
> And *feel* the steady candle-flame, and *taste*
> Good strong thick stupefying incense-smoke

suggests the level of his response. He enjoys the sensuous stimulus which art provides and he judges it by its monetary value or its size. He sneers at Gandolf's tomb because of its clammy paltriness, an antithesis to the rare and costly one which he plans for himself. Typically, he is more impressed by the size than the beauty of the lapis.

The Bishop's imagery, lacking in structural complexity, helps define his limitations. A subconscious expression of his deference to crude force and power ("As fresh-poured red wine of a mighty pulse," "Like God the Father's globe on both his hands," "stabbed me with ingratitude"), it is an ironic counterpart to his own weakness. Like other elements of structure, it is primarily sensuous, displaying his fascination with the physiological ("Jew's head cut off at the nape," "Madonna's breast," "eyes . . . as a lizard's quick," "great smooth marbly limbs"), the plastic, the tactile. His concern with these things when he himself is on the point of dissolution provides irony as well as an explanation of his desire to be embodied in a tomblike world.

The scene itself is pictorial and symbolic. The Bishop, arms folded, feet stretched forth, lies on his couch with the bedclothes for a mortcloth dropping around him in laps and folds of sculptor's-work. His sons, like columns, stand round his bed. There is in the situation a rigidity almost as if the old Bishop were actually as well as figuratively dead. As the poem develops, we sense a merging of the symbolic into the actual—with the important reservation that the imaginary tomb will never materialize.

Light is used here to suggest inner drama much as it is in "Fra Lippo Lippi" and "Andrea del Sarto." The Bishop is dying by slow degrees during the long hours of night, with his bed-bier lighted by tapers. Whatever vision he may claim is fitful and uncertain; his phantom-like being may at any moment be lost in darkness. As his hope wanes and death approaches, the candles are partly extinguished.

His imagery consists primarily of similes and personifications. Each serves an immediate purpose and together they express abstractly subterraneous currents in the Bishop's consciousness of which he is scarcely aware. Yet they fail to unite structurally with others in a complex relationship such as characterizes "Andrea del Sarto." A more complex pattern would be incongruous, of course, for the Bishop is incapable of dealing with the intricate kind of symbolism which Andrea's awareness opens for him; indeed, the Bishop's lack of self-understanding renders impossible such integration. It is his single vision which forms the ironic pattern of the poem. His imagery must operate within the narrow limits imposed by his intellectual and emotional awareness. He is concerned about life, success, and some ultimate destiny, and having found his *summum bonum* in the material and sensuous, he arrives at what to him is a satisfactory solution to his problem. Until the very end, he is disturbed neither by the frustrating knowledge that he has failed, nor by the more perplexing and unsolved problems which might stimulate a more sensitive individual.

In the passages spoken in semiconsciousness an inner superficiality parallels his surface brilliance. He seems only vaguely aware of the meaning of his quotations until circumstances force upon him the fact that life is vanity and man is mortal. The most revealing passage in the poem is

> The bas-relief in bronze ye promised me,
> Those Pans and Nymphs ye wot of, and perchance
> Some tripod, thyrsus, with a vase or so,
> The Savior at his sermon on the mount,
> St. Praxed in a glory, and one Pan
> Ready to twitch the Nymph's last garment off,
> And Moses with the tablets. . . .

Here pagan and Christian elements are indiscriminately brought together in a manner which to the moral judgment appears incongruous. The confusion seems largely to cancel what might otherwise appear the import of the questions, spoken also in semiconsciousness. The Bishop, however, apparently recognizes no inconsistency, accepting all as appropriate subjects for art. Thus the projected bas-relief is a symbolic expression of his standard of values, suggesting the superficial hold Christianity had on him. That it appears confused is consistent with the traits which I have already noted in his conduct. It should be stated again that Browning is not discussing morals didactically. Here, as in "The Statue and the Bust," he is concerned with a standard of values primarily as a psychological stimulus which produces action revelatory of character and situation.

That the Bishop created for himself a character and a world opposed to objective reality is clear. Before turning to the ironic pattern which brings these together in artistic form, I should like to note Browning's means of communication—through which, it seems to me, he made a distinctive contribution to poetic art.

In addition to presenting incident, narrative, and statement, he also communicates symbolically the complex emotions, sensations, and thoughts not yet formulated into rational phrases. The latter are expressed directly in their preconscious state unshaped by the rationalizing mind. The result is a disruption of normal syntax and an incoherency implicit in matter itself. Had the Bishop seen clearly enough to rationalize his confusion, his communication would have been different: a reflection upon, rather than an immediate sensuous and emotional expression of, experience. In using linguistic signs to express symbolically an area of experience not yet rendered totally conscious, Browning points toward the stream of consciousness technique of twentieth-century literature. Browning maintains the dramatic form, implying in the Bishop's speech a state which Joyce reports directly; it seems apparent, however, that each writer, in his own way, draws from a common source of experience. Browning's use of this method in much of his work beginning with *Sordello* accounts partly for what the Victorians called his obscurity.

Browning used this method for a number of reasons.

Here the two levels of communication parallel the two strata of meaning and make the reader more immediately conscious of discrepancies which form the basis of the poem's irony. The technique dramatizes the tensions between the cultured, superficial structure of the Bishop's own creation and the deeper reality of life itself. For Browning, it permitted a more precise expression of the actual experience he was trying to communicate. He struggled in all his poetry to find the exact structural equivalent for a complex poetic experience, and in his best works he succeeded. Marred as it is by immaturities, *Sordello* is yet one of Browning's poems with which we cannot dispense. His attempt to make structure a sensitive expression of meaning foreshadows what he later realized more successfully. His syntactical elements, fragments, associational items, and rapid transitions actually indicate the sensitive response of structure to matter in the joint task of expressing poetic meaning. The promises of *Sordello* are fulfilled in "The Bishop Orders His Tomb."

Let us note how the technique actually works in the poem. The Bishop makes a statement, but we understand by a complex of structural devices that there are other levels of meaning. In addition to reading words in normal syntactical order, we must read also word choice and distribution, sentence structure, omissions, punctuation, sound patterns, and rhythm; we must be responsive to emotional and sensuous stimuli; we must take the whole structural pattern as symbolic of a meaning not explicitly stated.

I have already shown how sound, diction, and imagery are immediately communicative. So are the incomplete sentences, associational fragments, and ellipses. There are two types of incompletions. One communicates experience directly in anacoluthic structure in order to gain imaginative, emotional, and sensuous immediacy:

—That's if ye carve my epitaph aright,
Choice Latin, picked phrase, Tully's every word,
No gaudy ware like Gandolf's second line—
Tully, my masters?

In addition to communicating ideas, these lines give also a direct impression of the rapidly changing flow of the Bishop's thoughts and feelings.

The other type of incompletion is the unfinished periodic:

My sons, ye would not be my death? Go dig
The white-grape vineyard where the oil-press stood,
Drop water gently till the surface sink,
And if ye find . . . Ah God, I know not, I! . . .
Bedded in store of rotten fig-leaves soft,
And corded up in a tight olive-frail,
Some lump, ah God, of *lapis lazuli*,
Big as a Jew's head cut off at the nape,
Blue as a vein o'er the Madonna's breast . . .
Sons, all have I bequeathed you, villas, all, . . .

And as yon tapers dwindle, and strange thoughts
Grow, with a certain humming in my ears,
About the life before I lived this life,
And this life too, popes, cardinals and priests,
Saint Praxed at his sermon on the mount,
Your tall pale mother with her talking eyes,
And new-found agate urns as fresh as day,
And marble's language, Latin pure, discreet,
—Aha, ELUCESCEBAT quoth our friend?

In neither case did the Bishop forget what he began to say. Either he realized that, having communicated his meaning, he needed say no more, or he was diverted by a more powerful stream of thought stimulated by association of ideas or by a response from his audience. Taken as a whole, the statements accurately express psychological phenomena even though their logic is faulty.

For example, he is reminded of the tragedy of possibly losing his lapis, which he would give his "all" to preserve. Impulsively he reminds his sons:

> Sons, all have I bequeathed you, villas, all,
> That brave Frascati villa with its bath,
> So, let the blue lump poise between my knees.

Again, in the sons' inattention, the Bishop suddenly realizes the futility of his hopes and abruptly ends his description of the tomb in an ellipsis that expresses more than words.

The associational fragment is an incompletion, but it differs from the others in that it is more fragmentary, less communicative on the language level, and is differently related to adjoining elements:

> Nephews—sons mine . . . ah God, I know not! Well—

> Peach-blossom marble all, the rare, the ripe
> As fresh-poured red wine of a mighty pulse.
> —Old Gandolf with his paltry onion-stone,
> Put me where I may look at him! True peach,
> Rosy and flawless: how I earned the prize!

> "Do I live, am I dead?" There, leave me, there!
> For ye have stabbed me with ingratitude

To death—ye wish it—God, ye wish it! Stone—
Gritstone, a-crumble! Clammy squares which sweat
As if the corpse they keep were oozing through—
And no more *lapis* to delight the world!

The unity of these sentences rests upon the associational relationship between their elements, or between their elements and some object, emotion, or sensation suggested by them. In the third example, for instance, the unity of the two sentences is emotional. The grief suggested by the first line links together the loss of the jasper and the baths. Their meaning encompasses the whole of the inner experience which they objectify. There are many such examples in "The Bishop Orders His Tomb."

The ellipsis functions also to communicate subconscious experience. In some cases it is indicated orthographically, but often it is not. In the poem, there are Browning's usual omissions of function words, and of even more important elements in the associational fragments. These, however, are not particularly disturbing to the reader. Readers who find "The Bishop Orders His Tomb" cryptic do so largely because of the omitted lines and paragraphs. They fail to see that the meaning may be emotional and sensuous, not always rational, and that much of it can be expressed better by what is not said than by what is. Browning might have gained readier intelligibility had he expanded, but in that case he would have done what Ruskin did—written thirty pages of prose. The real poem here is not contained within the one hundred and twenty-five lines, but rather in the complex world of thought, emotion, and experience which they represent. Through this manner of communication, a forerunner of the stream of consciousness,

Browning gains immediacy of expression without entering the poem in his own person. The reader not only understands what is said but comes to feel and sense the Bishop's world.

Irony serves in "The Bishop Orders His Tomb" the unifying function which imagery accomplishes for "Andrea del Sarto." It provides a means of bringing together the diverse ways of seeing. The central ironies result from a juxtaposition of the Bishop's high evaluation of himself and his actual insignificance when he comes to die; his illusion that he has controlled great wealth and the final discovery in the defection of his sons that his ownership is only temporary; his materialistic one-dimensional view of life and his grotesque desire for a kind of immortality; his pride in the exercise of authority and the realization of the ineffectualness of his "order."

Like so many other of Browning's poems, "The Bishop Orders His Tomb" is marked by a dialectical movement between juxtaposed opposites: from a stricture on vanity to a description of the elaborate tomb; from the peace of St. Praxed's to the tooth and nail fight with Gandolf; from the angels in the aery dome to the cursed carrion of old Gandolf in the tomb; from oozing corpse to lighted tapers. The direction of the poem is toward an ultimate identification by which the Bishop gains a surprising, ironic self-realization.

It is questionable whether at the beginning of the poem the Bishop realizes the full significance of the words "Vanity, saith the preacher, vanity!" for with apparent unawareness he proceeds directly to describe plans for an elaborate tomb. Both the title and the opening line counterpoint the Bishop's illusion against the reality. In the first, he is unaware of his limited power; in the second, of his own weakness. The poem provides the dramatic development of his discovery of both.

One of the ironic devices used throughout is the Bishop's quotations. They are precisely applicable to him, but any real meaning which they might have has been so submerged that it fails to operate on a conscious level. Like the priestly blessing which he gives his sons, they are echoes of ecclesiastical duties performed emptily in the past. Appearing only during his semiconscious moments, they convey more truth than he is able or willing to admit. The lines

> Swift as a weaver's shuttle fleet our years:
> Man goeth to the grave, and where is he?

are followed directly by

> Did I say basalt for my slab, sons? Black—
> 'T was ever antique-black I meant!

However, he does not yet realize how much death really will end for him. He displays a characteristic attitude in his reference to his sons' mother:

> . . . she is dead beside,
> Dead long ago, and I am Bishop since.

Weakness and death belong to his mistress and Gandolf, strength and life to him. He may confuse himself with God ("Like God the Father's globe . . .") but never with other men. It is an embittering blow, therefore, when he is brought at last to acknowledge the common tie, death, with his mistress and Gandolf. His frustrating impotency in the presence of death causes him to wonder whether life has not been a dream after all. For to him life had meant "tooth and nail" fighting, having his orders respected and obeyed. Now, in contrast, his strength and power are gone. "Do I live . . . ?" he asks. Passivity is certainly death. The Bishop's concept of life as activity is counterpointed by his actual powerlessness. We have both the Bishop of endless striving and animal activity, and the Bishop fossilized symbolically in marble.

The latter is the more basic and eventually predominates. Appropriately, therefore, there are in the poem fewer active verbs, more passive, than in either "Andrea del Sarto" or "Fra Lippo Lippi." Faced with the inevitability of death and fearing extinction, he turns to the tomb as a means of preserving his superiority and places his "order" with his sons.

From this point, the tension increases until the Bishop comes partly to realize about himself and the tomb what the reader has known from the beginning. The poem is a dramatic presentation of a self-revelation which forces the Bishop to accept a reality paradoxical to the illusion under which he has lived. More striking than the discrepancy between the tombs is his changing relationship with people and things, particularly with Gandolf. In the beginning he is triumphant and Gandolf is humiliated; in the conclusion the Bishop has been humbled and Gandolf relatively elevated. Gandolf won a minor triumph by dying early and securing for his tomb the best niche in the church, even though his resting place was marked by paltry onion-stone. "Put me where I may look at him," the Bishop gloats. In contrast, he muses, his tomb will be magnificent, his triumph final and com-

plete: "For Gandolf shall not choose but see and burst!"
Only gradually does he realize that he will not have his
wish. Instead of lapis to delight the world, there will be
only

> . . . Stone—
> Gritstone, a-crumble! Clammy squares which sweat
> As if the corpse they keep were oozing through—

Instead of reposing in luxury, he will

> . . . gasp
> Bricked o'er with beggar's mouldy travertine
> Which Gandolf from his tomb-top chuckles at!

The last line is the important one. The relative positions
of the Bishop and his old enemy have been reversed.

Further, the imagined tomb was a symbol of values
which the Bishop had considered enduring. It was to be
an appropriate summation of his achievements, embodying his cultural and material wealth. But instead, he receives the same cheap gritstone that marked Gandolf's
grave. After being feared and obeyed all his life, the
Bishop issues his last "order" only to discover that he has
no power to command. He tries to bribe his sons but
finds that what he offers has already passed from his
hands to theirs. Contrary to his supposition, power of
action lies with his sons, not with himself. At last he discovers what earlier had existed only vaguely in his subconscious: all, indeed, is vanity.

The final irony is in the line "Well go! I bless ye."
The Bishop has one thing in mind and makes the statement lightly. It has been part of his ecclesiastical duty to
give empty blessing, but unwittingly, it is no longer

empty. What he had once given nominally he now gives actually. Dying, he leaves "all" to his sons, and by his own definition of the good life he bestows on them the greatest blessing. It is doubly ironic that this, the first genuine blessing he has ever given, brings him no spiritual comfort.

V

Spiritual Dialectics:
Bishop Blougram's
Apology

"Bishop Blougram's Apology" is rarely considered one of Browning's best poems. Late Victorian critics condemned the Bishop for worldliness and found the poem lacking in "poeticality." Stopford Brooke says it is "perilously near the absence of poetry," [1] and G. K. Chesterton speaks of the Bishop as a "vulgar, fashionable priest, justifying his own cowardice over the comfortable wine and the cigars." [2] It has long been a critical commonplace to group the Bishop with Mister Sludge, Prince Hohenstiel, and Don Juan, and to dismiss them all as scoundrelly casuists, products of the prosaic side of Browning's talents. [3] It should be noted parenthetically, however, that the word *casuist* is not a derogatory term to Roman Catholics, as Chesterton has pointed out.

This popular judgment is inconsistent with Browning's interpretation of the poem as a not ungenerous portrayal of the Churchman, and, to some extent, inconsistent with the appraisal of Cardinal Wiseman, who is supposed to have provided the Bishop's prototype. [4] A

review of *Men and Women* in a Roman Catholic magazine, assumed to have been written by the Cardinal,
condemns the Bishop as "utterly mistaken in the very
ground work of religion," but concludes with the statement that "beneath the surface there is an undercurrent
of thought that is by no means inconsistent with our religion. . . ." [5]

Evidently, Browning did not consider as central
those elements which repelled later critics, and evidently
both he and the Cardinal read into the poem something
which others have missed. Some errors of the past may be
avoided if the poem is understood for what it is and
judged accordingly. It does not attempt to be a lyrical,
subjective expression of "high seriousness" in the manner of Tennyson and Arnold. It is, rather, a subtle, complex, witty presentation of character, situation, and argument. Its most distinguished quality is the manner in
which disparity, ambiguity, and irony are brought together to form an artistic whole. Part of the poem's
effectiveness comes from the balance achieved between
the forces generated, on the one hand, by the centrifugal
tendencies of the parts and, on the other, by the restrict-
ing and unifying power of poetic imagination.

Interest in the poem derives both from the drama
and the argument. An interpretation logically begins
with a discussion of the occasion, the speaker, and the
listener, the immediate stimuli for the argument. Bishop
Blougram is apologetic rather than dogmatic. He is not
delivering a sermon to the faithful, nor ostensibly is he
presenting an argument to convince skeptics in general.
He is addressing himself specifically to Gigadibs, a self-
professed literary man, a free-thinker, an idealist, who

assumes that the Bishop is either a fool or a knave, and who hopes to trap the prelate into making a sensational confession which he can turn into a profitable literary *exposé*.

Yet, there is dramatic weakness in this situation. Bishop Blougram is not arguing against an equal, say Comte or Fichte, but against one of their more incompetent followers, no match for the subtle Bishop. This, indeed, enervates the poem dramatically; still, from another point of view it is appropriate to Browning's purpose, making his attack double-edged. Dialectically, the Bishop argues against the ideas of his arch enemies (and only ostensibly against Gigadibs'); dramatically, he opposes himself to a further corruption of an already bad thing: its vulgar popularization by an insensitive, incompetent, blind follower. So the sacrifice of dramatic tension in the situation is compensated for by an increased richness in argument.

The Bishop is a complex character, incapable of being reduced to a simple type. He is torn psychologically between opposing forces, to both of which he owes some allegiance. Belief and uncertainty, strength and weakness are inextricably interwoven in his nature. Clearly, he is neither saint nor devil, but a man struggling hard to maintain faith in an age when to believe is difficult. Gigadibs, on the other hand, is a flat, one-dimensional figure whose emotional and mental incapacity has rendered him immune to the Bishop's conflicts. It is ironic that at the beginning of the poem Gigadibs mistakes weakness for strength and presents himself, in contrast to the Bishop, as the philosophical and moral superior. The poem develops by the technique of reversals already noted in "The Bishop Orders His Tomb." Part of its purpose is to right the errors of superficial judgment by deflating Gigadibs and by expanding the Bishop, each to his proper proportion. The young man's name is so grotesque as to suggest, perhaps too obviously, the Bishop's justly contemptuous attitude toward him. It is reminiscent of Carlyle's scornful coinage "Gigmanity" to designate rationalistic utilitarianism. I shall refer later to a similarity between one aspect of Bishop Blougram's and Carlyle's views of society.

Gigadibs imagines himself an enlightened skeptic who knows the new science and has read Strauss, Fichte, and Count D'Orsay. He has discarded revealed and institutional religion as a superstitious relic of the past, now acceptable only to fools and knaves. Intolerant of all external authority, political, social, or ecclesiastical, he talks about the dignity of man, the rightness of instincts, the necessity for individualism, and the challenge of the Ideal. Thus enlightened and emancipated, he looks upon the Bishop as an intellectual and moral inferior.

The Bishop's contrasting interpretation of the young man is acute and accurate, reveals incidentally a great deal about the Bishop himself, and, in juxtaposition to Gigadibs' own view, helps define the conflict between the two men. Actually, they are antithetical in every important way: the Bishop is a conservative, pragmatic defender of institutionalism; Gigadibs a liberal, idealistic advocate of a vague new order.

Sensitive to Gigadibs' egotism and prejudices, the Bishop proceeds indirectly, as he must, to expose the young man's affected pose. He seizes upon a contradiction between the idealistic creed which Gigadibs pro-

fesses and the more mundane one which he unwittingly
practices, proposing to reveal Gigadibs' double standard
and force him either to surrender his ideal or to reshape
his life to conform to it. The latter task the Bishop considers impossible, and it is one for which Gigadibs, as it
develops, has little relish.

Bishop Blougram first attacks Gigadibs' idealism as
providing an unrealistic basis for living.[6] In the cabin
figure he implies that the young man's position may serve
well as a parlor philosophy but that a more realistic attitude is required in the practical business of making a
comfortable life. Gigadibs himself admits as much in his
attitude toward the Bishop, whose low ideals he despises
but whose accomplishments he admires:

> And if I say, "despise me,"—never fear!
> I know you do not in a certain sense—
> Not in my arm-chair, for example: here,
> I well imagine you respect my place
> (*Status, entourage*, worldly circumstance)
> Quite to its value.

In contrast to Gigadibs, the Bishop interprets life in
terms of man's native limitations and circumstantial restrictions. Consequently, he treats Gigadibs' and his own
weakness with an honesty which, on one hand, places
him ideologically in the Christian tradition, and on the
other, allies him structurally with the French realists,
Balzac and Flaubert (the nineteenth-century writers
whom Browning admired most).[7]

Gigadibs, vague and superficial about basic issues,
is unable to systematize his thoughts. He mistakes non-
conformity for intellectuality. He is the young man

> . . . clever to a fault,
> The rough and ready man who writes apace,
> Reads somewhat seldomer, thinks perhaps even less—

and in the epilogue,

> (such they seemed
> Beside his interlocutor's loose cards
> Flung daily down, and not the same way twice).

The word *loose* characterizes, for the Bishop, Gigadibs'
thinking, and the phrase "loosed your mind" in the following fully expresses his contempt:

> . . . you would not be I.
> You would like better to be Goethe, now,
> Or Bounaparte, or, bless me, lower still,
> Count D'Orsay,—so you did what you preferred,
> Spoke as you thought, and, as you cannot help,
> Believed or disbelieved, no matter what,
> So long as on that point, whate'er it was,
> You loosed your mind, were whole and sole yourself.

Incapable of intellectual discipline, Gigadibs has
acquired a sleek modernity and parrots second-hand
ideas like a new convert. He fails to distinguish between
the merits of Goethe, Napoleon, and Count D'Orsay;
and, although he praises Goethe, he probably reads the
second-rate dandy and free thinker. His unsystematic
thinking helps shape the course of the argument which
follows, because it relieves the Bishop of the responsibility for developing a logical, coherent opposition, making his task largely a negative one. Gigadibs is boastful
of what he considers his intellectual independence. In

the nineteenth century he does not believe; yet, the
Bishop points out, in the Middle Ages he would have:

> How should you feel, I ask, in such an age,
> How act? As other people felt and did;
> With soul more blank than this decanter's knob,
> Believe—and yet lie, kill, rob, fornicate
> Full in belief's face, like the beast you'd be!

This judgment is both intellectual and moral. The Bishop
denies Gigadibs' capacity for individualism and charges
that in any age he would merely echo fashionable ideas.
Further, he asserts that Gigadibs' sense of right and
wrong is only a reflection of current social taboos. Actually, it is the Bishop who stands out against the popular
judgment of his age. If, then, individualism is meritorious,
the Bishop outweighs Gigadibs.

Gigadibs' priggishly superior and self-righteous attitude makes him particularly offensive to the Bishop. He
is also personally and socially crude. His naïve assump-
tion, for example, that under the influence of wine the
Bishop will be induced to make a sensational confession
of hypocrisy is insulting more for the boorish familiarity
which it presumes than for the intemperance which it
implies.

This, then, is the situation. Gigadibs has passed judgment upon the Bishop, and he is waiting for the sensational confirmation, the lurid details which will give zest
to the article he wishes to write. To his confusion and
to that of many readers, the Bishop appears inconsistently
co-operative:

> I promised, if you'd watch a dinner out,
> We'd see truth dawn together?—truth that peeps

Over the glasses' edge when dinner's done,
And body gets its sop and holds its noise
And leaves soul free a little.

But he implies more here than he appears on the surface
to say, employing a technique which characterizes the
entire poem. Truth has at least two faces—the Bishop
will indeed expose himself, but he will also expose
Gigadibs. The result will be sensational, but in an un-
expectedly ironical manner, for the young man will come
to see himself and the Bishop from a startlingly new perspective.

The poem falls into four sections (and an epilogue),
and in each the Bishop acts a different part. There are
the introduction (ll.1–173) in which he is superficially
the genial host and the skeptical, worldly clergyman; the
argument on Gigadibs' premises (174–554), in which as
casuist he attempts more to expose Gigadibs than to defend himself; the homily (555–748), in which as priest he
argues for the faith; and finally, the exposure (749–970),
in which as an affronted man he demolishes his would-be
detractor.

If "Bishop Blougram's Apology" is not one of
Browning's best poems, it is certainly one of his most
original. It is not distinctive for its idea, however. Most
Victorian poets were concerned about the problem of
religious belief, and all were acutely aware of the difficulty of reconciling faith with the new scientific ra-
tionalism. "Bishop Blougram's Apology" has in common
with *In Memoriam*, for example, the renunciation of
reason in deference to faith as a basis for religious certainty, although the Bishop is more intellectually skeptical than Tennyson. Tennyson wavers between total

skepticism ("We have but faith, we cannot know") and an eclecticism that makes the new science subservient to religious ends. The Bishop, on the other hand, humiliates the reason completely, espousing with utter disrespect for science the most difficult-to-believe miracles, the liquefaction of St. Januarius' blood and the winking virgin.

The Bishop's anti-intellectualism is not to be confused with primitivism or emotionalism. Rousseau and the Romantics may urge a return to primitive instincts, and Tennyson and Arnold may seek refuge in emotionality (*In Memoriam*, "Dover Beach"); the Bishop, however, insists upon the will to believe as being the basis for religion ("If you desire faith—then you've faith enough"). He belongs actually in a long line of intellectual skeptics which includes Montaigne, Sir Thomas Browne, Pascal, Dryden, Swift, Newman, and Chesterton, all brilliant and subtle men, distrustful of reason. So while he renounces the mind, the poem, paradoxically, is characterized by a dry intellectuality which many readers find unpoetical.

Its distinctiveness lies in its manner, which brings to the common problem a different sensibility, creating for it a peculiar sensuous and emotional context. Its subtle casuistry, wit, irony, and paradox place it, like "Fra Lippo Lippi," in that class of poetry which Arnold considers the product of wit. It is one of the few serious, unapologetically humorous poems of the Victorian period. "Bishop Blougram's Apology" is frankly argumentative, but differs from the work of older poets—Dryden's, for example—because of its greater intellectual and emotional complexity. Browning, avoiding simple generalizations straightforwardly presented, recognizes complexities and

describes the mind within an emotional and sensuous context in the process of formulating ideas. The result is
an argument that is psychological, intellectual, and sometimes ambiguous.

An apparent dichotomy between thought and emotion is a characteristic of "Bishop Blougram's Apology."
There are two important things to note about the prelate: he has subordinated mind in order to maintain faith,
and as a result, has achieved a life in which there are
more moments of belief than of disbelief. Because of his
character and the situation, the intellectual seems to out-
weigh the emotional in the poem, giving rise to the
quality which Brooke finds objectionable. Characteristic
is its constantly shifting point of view, its series of
charges and countercharges, its techniques of juxtaposition and ironic reversals. The Bishop's objective is established for him. He must expose Gigadibs to himself and
at the same time defend his own character and faith. Although he realizes even more clearly than Gigadibs that
it is difficult to believe, he is convinced that his final position is sounder than the agnostic's. To argue, however, on
the basis of faith and institutionalism would result on his
part in failure to communicate, and on Gigadibs' in further charges of fraud and hypocrisy. He must find some
common ground, then, on which they both may stand
temporarily. His solution involves him in subtleties which
many readers fail to recognize as the only possible means,
under the circumstances, to the desired end.

His method suggests one which Cardinal Newman
was often forced to adopt.[8] In section two he magnani-
mously agrees to argue from his opponent's premise, and
the ambivalence of his position makes it difficult to dis-

tinguish his own views from those which he temporarily assumes. His apology is actually an *argumentum ad hominem*.

Throughout the poem he shifts from one to the other as the occasion demands; but, on the whole, he is speaking from the assumed position in lines 174–554 and from his own in lines 555–748. Of course, the matter is complicated by the Bishop's extraordinarily complex nature. He has unquestionably experienced doubt and cynical negation which he expresses; he finds it difficult to believe; he prefers to enjoy the good things of life. His awareness of duality makes him competent to speak from either position.

His shifting point of view is illustrated by the Bishop's answer to Gigadibs' charge that he is worldly and gross. First accepting the young man's premise, the prelate excuses himself on the grounds that if religion lacks reality man has no choice but to be beastly. "Grant I'm a beast, why, beasts must live beasts' lives!" As quickly as he has made his point, however, he shifts positions, and from another point of view, obviously his own, rejects the whole charge:

> But, friend, I don't acknowledge quite so fast
> I fail of all your manhood's lofty tastes
> Enumerated so complacently.

Similarly, he seems initially to compromise his position by agreeing that it is impossible to believe wholeheartedly and that an imperfect faith may not be worth having. Immediately, however, he faces about ("Softly, my friend! I must dispute that point . . .") and effectively demonstrates the positive value of even an imperfect faith.

His strategy is to encourage Gigadibs to commit himself to an extreme position and then to turn his argument against him in the form of a countercharge. Gigadibs would dismiss belief because it cannot be held "fixedly, / Absolutely, and exclusively." Arguing from the same premise, the Bishop discredits unbelief because it too cannot be held without occasional wavering. He accepts Gigadibs' contention that a man's belief must be judged by the action which it produces, only to demonstrate the incompatibility of agnosticism and a life of action. By subtle dialectical manipulation he forces Gigadibs, finally, to admit that the real question is not whether a man will believe but what he will believe.

When Gigadibs offers to defend Martin Luther's enthusiasm against institutionalism, the Bishop points out that Luther's work has been done, unless, of course, his was the first in a series of rebellions against church authority which can terminate only when that authority is destroyed. If that were his mission, Strauss becomes his follower, and even Fichte who, after trimming away all that his enlightened mind finds repulsive, makes his "clever cut at God himself." The Bishop refuses to become part of such a company and rejects the suggestion that he purify his faith of excrescences. Once any element of a supernatural religion is sacrificed because it is irrational, he contends, the whole structure is threatened:

> I trust nor hand nor eye nor heart nor brain
> To stop betimes: they all get drunk alike.
> The first step, I am master not to take.

Having destroyed Gigadibs' favorite premises, he can argue for a positive acceptance of Christianity on the grounds that it best meets man's instinctive need for God, and for orthodoxy because it renders the church most effective.

His summary statement in defense of the faith sounds more like William James than St. Thomas.[9] He claims that objective certitude is impossible, not even desirable; that believing is first an act of will or desire; that faith in a thing helps create the thing itself; that the final test of truth lies in the consequences which it produces; that religion is a positive good and desirable because of what it does for the believer.

Although used throughout the poem, the technique of juxtaposition is particularly effective in the introductory section. The Bishop's initial strategy is to pretend compromise, invite Gigadibs' confidence, inflate his ego, and secure his commitment to an extreme position. Temporarily, he accepts the role created for him by Gigadibs and plays it with good-natured irony.

The reader's mind is required constantly to shift back and forth within the poem and to recognize disparate points of view, to make associations, and to interpret ironies. One of the Bishop's first statements appears particularly damaging to him:

> These long hot ceremonies of our church
> Cost us a little—oh, they pay the price,
> You take me—amply pay it!

A few lines later it is given a new perspective when the Bishop, forming Gigadibs' thoughts, has the young man say patronizingly:

He's quite above their humbug in his heart,
Half said as much, indeed—the thing's his trade. . . .

The tone of this at least modifies and enlarges the implications of the first.

The Bishop's love for comfort is placed in contrast with the simpler, more austere tastes which Gigadibs professes:

So, drawing comfortable breath again,
You weigh and find, whatever more or less
I boast of my ideal realized,
Is nothing in the balance when opposed
To your ideal, your grand simple life,
Of which you will not realize one jot.
I am much, you are nothing; you would be all,
I would be merely much: you beat me there.

The cabin figure is only partly serious and is intended primarily to get from Gigadibs a commitment to an ascetic philosophy which the Bishop can attack later as a sham, hiding the young man's real desires, which are not so different from those he condemns in the clergyman.

Similarly, he juxtaposes his intellectual and religious position against Gigadibs' primarily to evoke from him a pledge to personal honesty and an expression of distaste for all pretense, all half-hearted, half-lived-up-to ideals:

No dogmas nail your faith; and what remains
But say so, like the honest man you are?

These devices, the shifting point of view, the transformation of charge into countercharge, and ironic juxtaposition, are both material and structural. The effect which they create is heightened by an appropriate and harmonious use of sentence structure, rhythm, and diction.

Bishop Blougram's sentences do not wander aimlessly like Andrea's, are neither rushed impetuously by thought like Fra Lippo's nor halted and broken by confusion like those of the Bishop of St. Praxed's. Their carefully controlled and deftly manipulated structure reflects the greater calmness and rationality of Bishop Blougram's mind.

They are relatively short and less frequently elliptical. The Bishop's subtlety is reflected in the numerous subordinations arising out of his keen perception of relations and his ability to move quickly from major to minor premise. Falling into relatively short units which may terminate anywhere within the line, the sentences provide the proper medium for expressing the rapidly changing point of view and the subtle countercharges.

There are more questions and exclamations in "Bishop Blougram's Apology" than in any other poem included in this study, with the possible exception of "Saul." The Bishop's questions, unlike Andrea's, are real ones addressed directly to a listener with the full expectation of an answer. They signify the ambivalence of his own experience and are materially and structurally a part of his apologetic strategy. Short and pointed, they are not mere reflections of inner searchings and uncertainties seeking to evade rather than face honest answers. Their clarity and force signify that, in spite of his doubts, the Bishop is basically an honest man; he has conscientiously sought answers to his questions.

The numerous exclamations are rhetorically correlative with the questions. Their purpose is neither emotional nor psychological, but conceptual. They do not attempt to complete vaguely conceived emotional impressions or to push the reader from the finite into the infinite; they are rather the inevitable termination of beliefs positively expressed. The Bishop has rationalized his problems and arrived at some definite solutions, although to Gigadibs his performance somewhat resembles that of a tightrope walker. His own sense that he is walking on the "dangerous edge of things" is reflected in the quick, nervous movement of the cadence and in the short, pointed rhetorical units, but he does keep his balance. Actually, he shows amazing confidence which is more than mere bravado, a remarkable fact in view of the difficulties which he has experienced:

> What matter though I doubt at every pore,
> Head-doubts, heart-doubts, doubts at my fingers' ends,
> Doubts in the trivial work of every day,
> Doubts at the very bases of my soul
> In the grand moments when she probes herself—
> If finally I have a life to show,
> The thing I did, brought out in evidence
> Against the thing done to me underground
> By hell and all its brood, for aught I know?

Of course, the ultimate expression of his confidence comes in his acceptance of Pascal's great wager of his life against there being a God.

There is close correlation between the metrical rhythm, the conversational cadence, and the sense of the line. "Bishop Blougram's Apology" is the most nearly regular of all the poems included here, with the possible exception of "Saul." But two poems could scarcely be more unlike than these. There is no "musicality" in "Bishop Blougram's Apology," no disturbing conflicts between meter and idea. The triple alliance between meter, cadence, and sense creates a colloquial realism that gives significance and force to every statement the Bishop makes. It serves as a strong unifying device both by helping create a medium through which conflict may be clearly expressed and by providing at the same time an instrument for their reconciliation.

Similarly, the diction is primarily conceptual in its appeal, being heavily substantive and verbal. Bishop Blougram's nouns are mainly abstract. There is a close relation between those most frequently used and the philosophical and theological ideas of the poem. They reflect areas of thought which most concern the Bishop, pose tensions which he has struggled to reconcile: *life, faith, doubt, God, truth, soul, unbelief*. Those of definite religious significance have meaning immediately apparent. His concern with the end which a line of thought or an action produces, his pragmatic interest in religion, pervades everything he says and is appropriately suggested in the frequently used words *way* and *end*. Less trustful of impulse than Gigadibs, the Bishop has a deep respect for law as it operates both in traditionalism and institutionalism.

The dichotomy in the poem between thought and emotion is Blougram's, not necessarily Browning's. It has dramatic relevancy providing a basic clue for interpreting the Bishop, who, unable to reconcile mind and spirit, has accepted their duality and established between them a balance that enables him to maintain faith. That which the rational mind cannot do, the will or the desire to believe must. Through the exercise of this faculty the Bishop achieves wholeness occasionally, as I shall suggest later. "Bishop Blougram's Apology" is indeed different from Donne's poems in its greater objectivity, but it is no less an artistic whole. Its structure is the correlative of its matter, both uniting to present the complex meaning of the poem. Basically, it is the Bishop, not the poem, that is dichotomized.

It must be emphasized that it is a dissociation of emotion from concept and not an absence of emotion that is found in the poem, indeed, that occasionally the Bishop attains a level of experience in which the dichotomy momentarily disappears altogether. Because of the situation, emotional passages appear as little more than asides, but they indicate that the Bishop is capable of insight and feeling. He may love life's comforts, but he is also sensitive to its beauty and spirit:

> Just when we are safest, there's a sunset-touch,
> A fancy from a flower-bell, some one's death,
> A chorus-ending from Euripides,—
> And that's enough for fifty hopes and fears
> As old and new at once as nature's self,
> To rap and knock and enter in our soul,
> Take hands and dance there, a fantastic ring,
> Round the ancient idol, on his base again,—
> The grand Perhaps!

Admitting his deficiency in Martin Luther's kind of enthusiasm, his religion, at the same time, is to him the expression of a vital relationship, a union between man and God, and ultimately a matter of faith and feeling:

You own your instincts? why, what else do I,
Who want, am made for, and must have a God
Ere I can be aught, do aught?—no mere name
Want, but the true thing with what proves its truth,
To wit, a relation from that thing to me,
Touching from head to foot—which touch I feel,
And with it take the rest, this life of ours!

All's doubt in me; where's break of faith in this?
It is the idea, the feeling and the love,
God means mankind should strive for and show forth
Whatever be the process to that end,—
And not historic knowledge, logic sound,
And metaphysical acumen, sure!
"What think ye of Christ," friend? when all's done
    and said,
Like you this Christianity or not?

His remarks on doubt are poignant and sincere, in-
dicating the intensity of his struggles:

(Greek endings, each the little passing-bell
That signifies some faith's about to die)

                              . . . the child
Feels God a moment, ichors o'er the place,
Plays on and grows to be a man like us.

        Pure faith indeed—you know not what you ask!
Naked belief in God the Omnipotent,
Omniscient, Omnipresent, sears too much
The sense of conscious creatures to be borne.

What matter though I doubt at every pore,
Head-doubts, heart-doubts, doubts at my fingers' ends,
Doubts in the trivial work of every day,
Doubts at the very bases of my soul.

Gigadibs accuses him of charlatanry, and the Bishop does sometimes argue on grounds of expedience; he has nevertheless a sense of reverence and awe, apparent in the following:

> It's like those eerie stories nurses tell,
> Of how some actor on a stage played Death,
> With pasteboard crown, sham orb and tinselled dart,
> And called himself the monarch of the world;
> Then, going in the tire-room afterward,
> Because the play was done, to shift himself,
> Got touched upon the sleeve familiarly,
> The moment he had shut the closet door,
> By Death himself. Thus God might touch a Pope
> At unawares, ask what his baubles mean,
> And whose part he presumed to play just now?

The words suggest Gigadibs but the spirit is Blougram's. Because he does believe, he speaks with repugnance of hypocritical pretense.

The Bishop, although the young man considers him self-indulgent and contemptuous of mankind, is stirred to anger by the thought of Napoleon's brutal conquests, and is scornful of Gigadibs' idolatry of this man of action:

> . . . we do see
> The blown-up millions—spatter of their brains
> And writhing of their bowels and so forth,
> In that bewildering entanglement
> Of horrible eventualities
> Past calculation to the end of time!
> Can I mistake for some clear word of God
> (Which were my ample warrant for it all)
> His puff of hazy instinct, idle talk?

The Bishop is a traditionalist, an institutionalist, a believer in hierarchical government (in the way that Samuel Johnson and Edmund Burke were; and, in a sense, as Carlyle, who speaks of society as a "mystical, miraculous, unfathomable Union," [10] was), which means that his desires are for a companionable relationship with mankind. The apparent harshness in his statements about ruling the masses is ironical, for he can imagine nothing more inhumane than Gigadibs' uncompromising, depersonalizing idealism. For individualism and personal isolationism he would substitute a hierarchical relationship which would bring all men together.

These passages, isolated from the rest of the poem, have been praised by adverse critics as being in themselves poetic. And they are. Not only are they warmly emotional and, many of them, lyrical in effect, but they contain some of the most effective imagery in Browning. For example, the terrifying sense of the Real in the tireroom after the play is over reveals the shoddiness of make-believe and takes us close to the meaning of the poem in a way that belongs peculiarly to the finest poetry. It is difficult, in fact, to imagine expression of intellectual states—doubt and faith—more sensuously and emotionally effective than those in some of these lines.

Yet, apart from the whole these passages have little artistic significance, for they must be either indispensable to the poem or artistic mistakes. Their imagery functions significantly only within the framework of the whole poem, suggesting that on rare occasions the Bishop succeeds in unifying his sensibilities and in achieving a wholeness of religious experience. Dialectically, they serve both to deny Gigadibs' charges and to give complexity and depth to the Bishop's character. Without the qualities which these suggest, he would be flat indeed. When he is seen in all his complexity, Chesterton's interpretation is recognized as unsatisfactory, both because of its oversimplifications and its wrong emphasis.

In "Bishop Blougram's Apology" we have a situation that occurs so often in Browning's work that it might be called archetypal: idealism and cynicism meet in one man or one situation. Such is the case in *The Ring and the Book*, a work which imperceptive critics have rendered sentimental by noting only the beautiful and idealistic traits of Pompilia, Caponsacchi, and the Pope. Browning, however, was aware also of the ugly and evil in Guido and the lawyers and refused the advice of his friend Julia Wedgwood to modify his treatment of them.[11] The tension between these forces and man's inability—even the Pope's—always to act unhesitatingly upon them gives to Browning's masterpiece its distinctive characteristics. His awareness of the co-existence of good and evil and beauty and ugliness in all life and his struggle to reconcile and order them makes him inevitably an ironist on the cosmic scale.

Although few of Browning's poems contain so many disparate elements as "Bishop Blougram's Apology," when all devices, structural and material, are viewed in their intrinsic relationship, they are recognized as forming a unity impressively meeting the requirements of a successful poem. Any disagreement about the merits of "Bishop Blougram's Apology" must soon degenerate into a quarrel over the relative merits of dramatic-wit poetry and subjective-lyrical poetry.

Bishop Blougram concludes his main argument with

the third section, but Gigadibs still has another truth to see. A man with greater sensitiveness would already have guessed the implications of the Bishop's argument, but Gigadibs must be shown more clearly. Consequently, the Bishop lays aside his role as casuist and priest and speaks directly as a man in terms that Gigadibs can understand. The revelation which follows clarifies things which have been suggested earlier, and throws light upon the Bishop's argument and method by revealing the extent to which they are ironic. Gigadibs is judged by his own standards and found to be

> . . . as much a slave as I,
> A liar, conscious coward and hypocrite,
> Without the good the slave expects to get,
> In case he has a master after all!

The Bishop's final sketch of Gigadibs is a harsh one: the young interviewer writes "statedly" for *Blackwood's Magazine;* he does insignificant literary criticism in a manner derivative from the Germans; his greatest triumph is one story in imitation of Dickens which amuses the Bishop for a whole month. The confident young man who approached the Bishop with an attitude of moral and intellectual superiority is completely disarmed. The Bishop's final blow is to challenge him to publish what he has learned and to offer his influence in getting his second-rate articles printed in church magazines.

Thus, the Bishop has "smiled and talked" for an hour. His purpose has been to deflate Gigadibs and, incidentally, to defend his own character and faith. Although he cannot wholeheartedly approve the methods he has used, he has met the exigencies of the situation and is consoled by the fact that he has in reserve a better defense of religion should he be called upon to present it:

> "I justify myself
> On every point where cavillers like this
> Oppugn my life: he tries one kind of fence,
> I close, he's worsted, that's enough for him.
> He's on the ground: if ground should break away
> I take my stand on, there's a firmer yet
> Beneath it, both of us may sink and reach. . . ."

The Bishop's argument, then, is a *tour de force*, not intended as the ultimate defense of the Christian position. Within its more limited objective—the demonstration of the pragmatic superiority of religion over agnosticism even on rationalistic grounds—it is surprisingly effective. Although Gigadibs was not converted to Roman Catholicism, the Bishop succeeded in making untenable the young man's position:

> Just a week
> Sufficed his sudden healthy vehemence. . . .
> And having bought, not cabin-furniture
> But settler's-implements (enough for three)
> And started for Australia—there, I hope,
> By this time he has tested his first plough,
> And studied his last chapter of St. John.

VI

Spiritual Dogmatics:
Saul

"Saul" has always been one of Browning's most popular poems. It was early admired by the Pre-Raphaelites and later by members of the Rhymers' Club. It was regarded also with special reverence by the London Browning Society. As a result of its almost universal acceptance, "Saul" has probably the longest bibliography of any of Browning's shorter poems.

The late nineteenth century was obviously attracted by its melody and its lush diction and imagery. Arthur Symons says of it: "Music, song, the beauty of nature, the joy of life, the glory and greatness of man, the might of Love, human and divine: all these are set to an orchestral accompaniment of continuous harmony, now hushed as the wind among the woods at evening, now strong and sonorous as the storm-wind battling with the mountain pine." [1]

The Browning Society admired it for entirely different reasons. In 1889 Miss Anna M. Stoddart read before the London Browning Society a paper [2] in which she gave the poem a theological and moral interpretation generally accepted by subsequent societies. George Bernard Shaw, then a member of the London organization, was so repelled by Miss Stoddart's interpretation that he began a quarrel, more personal than aesthetic, productive of such ill feelings that someone moved the dissolution of the society.

The reputation of the poem has been so firmly established that a number of literary historians, it appears, have accepted it without close critical consideration. A recent history, for example, has this to say:

Perhaps the best known poem through which to approach Browning, after the comparatively easy "Rabbi Ben Ezra," is "Saul." Written in smooth, for him unusually smooth, anapaestic measure, it contains more delightful imagery than is common with him, is as dramatic as anything that he wrote, and reveals as clearly as any of his works his conception of spiritual values attained by the perpetual warring in life.[8]

Present taste is less responsive to the qualities for which Symons praised "Saul," and its theological merits alone no longer seem a reason for admiring it. I suggest that a fresh assessment of its literary merits will permit an evaluation of the poem for what it actually is.

One is immediately impressed by a twofold recognition. First, there is an element in "Saul" either not present or latent in Browning's earlier poetry, an element not entirely justified by the rest of the poem. Second, in "Saul," unlike other poems in this study, the poet's objective is not entirely clear. I shall deal with these two problems in turn.

The golden-haired child, the lilies, the harp, the dew, the religious fervor, the Pre-Raphaelite imagery,

the lush diction, the sensuous, sweet rhythm are characteristics not found generally in Browning's poetry. Their
presence here is somewhat puzzling. DeVane thinks that
Browning wrote under the influence of Christopher
Smart; and, indeed, there are numerous passages in the
poem which suggest "A Song to David." [4] But probably
even more explanatory is the fact that in January of
1845—the month in which he began "Saul"—Robert
Browning discovered the poetry of Elizabeth Barrett,
which he enthusiastically praised for "the fresh strange
music, the affluent language, the exquisite pathos, and
the brave new thought. . . ." [5]

These are precisely the characteristics of "Saul"
which are new in Browning's poetry. This suggestion of
Elizabeth Barrett's influence is not merely speculative;
there is evidence to substantiate it. "Saul" reflects both
the spirit and technique of Miss Barrett's "The Soul
Travelling," "Earth and Her Praise," "A Song Against
Singing," and "A Rhapsody of Life's Progress." Close
parallels between lines in the latter and in "Saul" have
been noted by Betty Miller.[6] Take for example these
lines from "A Rhapsody of Life's Progress":

> And we run with the stag, and we leap with the horse,
> And we swim with the fish through the broad water-
>   course,
> And we strike with the falcon, and hunt with the hound,
> And the joy which is in us flies out with a wound.
> And we shout so aloud, "We exult, we rejoice,"
> That we lose the low moan of our brothers around;
> And we shout so adeep down creation's profound,
>   We are deaf to God's voice.

The spirit, the meter, even the diction and syntax are

similar to those of "Saul," particularly in section nine; Browning obviously wrote the first nine sections (published separately as a fragment in 1845) under the influence of Miss Barrett. I shall refer to this subject again.

The second problem is central to the poem's interpretation. There is in "Saul" a strange uncertainty, a confused sense of direction. What is its purpose? It might be to develop dramatically a character and situation; it might be to express ideas either for themselves (as in *La Saisaz*, in which case the poem would be didactic, not dramatic), or as materials to provoke character revelation (as in "Fra Lippo Lippi" and "Bishop Blougram's Apology," in which case it might be either didactic or dramatic); it might be to communicate lyrically (as in mystical poetry) a religious experience. Either would be poetically legitimate and, properly executed, artistically successful. Let us determine first which of these the poem attempts and, second, appraise the artistic success with which each is achieved.

It should be emphasized that "Saul" is not a dramatic monologue, nor is it satisfactorily a soliloquy. Strictly speaking, it is a narrative report of the meeting between Saul and David. And while we cannot require of it the dialectical interplay between characters which we find, for example, in "Andrea del Sarto," we may rightfully expect that it meet the dramatic standards implicit in good narrative poetry (Batho and Dobrée claim that it does). This much may be said: it begins with a situation as dramatic as that in "Fra Lippo Lippi" and "The Bishop Orders His Tomb"; it maintains a pretense of objectivity up to the last stanza; it develops through a series of actions and conversations. Certainly, the necessary conditions for "the development of a soul" are present.

Yet it is a dramatic failure that Browning's interest is not clearly focused on either Saul or David. In the beginning, both title and situation suggest that Saul is the central character. This is also implied by Abner's statement:

> . . . "Since the King, O my friend, for thy counte-
> nance sent,
> "Neither drunken nor eaten have we; nor until from
> his tent
> "Thou return with the joyful assurance the King liveth
> yet,
> "Shall our lips with the honey be bright, with the water
> be wet. . . ."

Saul's psychical restoration and his return to the army seem the chief purpose of the poet. It is a purpose, however, which he never clearly accomplishes.

What actually happens to Saul? In stanza seven he shows signs of awakening, but his salvation at this point is incomplete, since he has attained only a state something like Carlyle's "center of indifference." In stanza fifteen he is sufficiently restored to make an affectionate and moving gesture toward David. We feel that the climax is near and that something decisive will happen to the King. But the force of the situation becomes operative upon David, not Saul, and the course of the entire poem is redirected. This makes possible David's vision of Christ, which produces the state of religious exaltation communicated in the concluding section of the poem, but the effect of the fuller vision upon Saul and his problem is never related. The title, indeed, seems inapt to the poem as it is finally finished. The dramatic failure here is apparent. "Saul" has one beginning, a confused middle, and a different ending.

Not only is the action undramatic, but so is the structure. The last section, the only part of the poem that is genuinely a soliloquy, might be considered legitimately an epilogue. The rest of the poem, however, maintains a pretense of dramatic form. The first three sections are introductory narrative; those following, a report of the meeting between Saul and David. The songs and the argument are reported "conversation," not meditative reflections upon experience. They are advanced first exploratively to discover Saul's need, and later directed specifically to meet it. Clearly the climactic lines

". . . O Saul, it shall be
"A Face like my face that receives thee; a Man like
to me,
"Thou shall love and be loved by, for ever: a Hand
like this hand
"Shall throw open the gates of new life to thee! See
the Christ stand!"

maintain to the end the illusion of a dramatic situation. Further, the rapport between the characters is once convincing—in the scene at the conclusion of section fifteen.

Yet, the dramatic front seems false. The poem is paper drama. Expectations aroused in the first few stanzas are never satisfied: the direction of the action gets lost; Saul, initially presented with individuality, soon becomes merely an object for David to speak at, not with;

David steals his own show. In short, the tension required of dramatic narrative is lacking in both situation and character.

If, rejecting the poem as the development of a dramatic situation, we look for its centrality in the vision of the latter sections, David becomes the chief character, induced to self-portraiture through his reaction to a body of ideas. Such an interpretation would render the poem either didactic or psychological. Evaluation from this point of view requires a brief explanation of the ideas and of David's response to them.

The greatest difficulty in accepting the poem as a psychological study is that David is no more clearly developed than Saul. He seems to have been taken from one of Elizabeth Barrett's poems and placed incongruously in a Browning situation. Or, it might appear that he is an expression of what Empson calls the nineteenth-century child cult.[7] If this were the case, Browning would be placing himself in the "pastoral" tradition which, basically, goes back to Virgil and which was alternately revived and lost many times before Wordsworth reestablished it in the nineteenth century.

Once before Browning had chosen a child, Pippa, as central character; and in some respects Pippa and David are alike. David's "How good is man's life, the mere living . . ." duplicates the naïve simplicity of Pippa's "God's in his heaven— / All's right with the world" as statement of primitive and unsophisticated innocence. But the similarity of the characters and of the poems is only superficial. Pippa is a fully developed and consistent child character, while David is neither convincingly child nor man. *Pippa Passes* is saved from sentimentality by its conflicts and ironies, by the wholeness of its intellectual system, qualities which are not present in "Saul." Pippa's simplicity is given perspective by the larger, more complex framework of the poem; David, on the other hand, remains unsatisfyingly one-dimensional.

Further, Browning's own presence is more keenly felt in "Saul" than in *Pippa Passes*. Sections sixteen through eighteen seem Browning's response to his wife's advice to "speak out of that personality which God made. . . ." It is disturbing, however, because often the poet's voice is so loud that we can scarcely hear David, the ostensible speaker.

Of course, David could not be censured for lacking the sophistication of Bishop Blougram if he were convincingly the child-philosopher, but certainly it is a dramatic flaw to present him in the external trappings of a primitive shepherd boy and then have him speak as a rationalistic defender of theological dogma. His apology for the Incarnation in sections sixteen through eighteen is psychologically unrealistic.

It should be noted, however, that here, as in his other poems, Browning attempts to give religious truth psychological rather than doctrinal significance. Yet the indefiniteness of his intellectual system is inevitably disturbing. It is difficult to know precisely what he means by the Incarnation, and one looks in vain for its logical counterpart, the Atonement. (The symbolic suggestion of Saul in the Christ role only adds confusion.) One suspects that the poet himself accepted the Incarnation as a symbolic or mythical expression of God's love for man rather than as an actual historical occurrence. The poem, charged with familiar sentiments and laden with traditional symbolism, raises expectations that are not wholly met—expectations which make it impossible to justify the poem's vagueness as prophecy dimly seen. Certainly, David sees too much (and that through the eyes of a nineteenth-century rationalist) to be considered seriously historical. Further, not only his thought, but his diction, his imagery, and his speech rhythm are wholly unlike that of the Biblical David whom we know through the Psalms.

In most of his poems Browning's own attitude is unimportant, for he advances dogma not to make his readers believe, but to make his characters feel and become believable. This is largely true, for example, of "Christmas Eve" and "Easter Day." His purpose in "Saul," however, is not clear. The effect upon David of his discovery of religious truth is not entirely unconvincing; yet it is difficult to reconcile the experience itself with the vaguely conceived character of the child-theologian. To whom does the vision belong—the shepherd boy or the apologist? Or Browning? Dramatic and psychological ineptness permits the poem to become as nearly didactic as anything Browning wrote. That didacticism is particularly offensive because the poet's vague theological system causes him to rely primarily upon sentimental emotionalism for his effect.

Browning, not often wrong in his analysis of character, is confused here. He himself complained of his difficulty to Elizabeth Barrett—whereupon she replied:

But your "Saul" is unobjectionable as far as I can see, my dear friend. He was tormented by an evil spirit—but how, we are not told . . . and the consolation is not obliged to be definite, . . . is it? [8]

This statement emphasizes a difference between the two poets. Elizabeth is undisturbed by the problem which Saul's condition presents to Browning's more analytical mind. She accepts unquestioningly the state as one produced by an "evil spirit" just as later she was to accept spiritualism. She suggests a consolation that, judging from her remark and her own poetry, is religious—even mystical—yet is only remotely applicable to the problem, which, as Browning conceived it, was psychological. Her treatment de-emphasized the conflicts characteristic of Browning's best work, providing an arbitrary solution which, in fact, is no solution at all, since it evades the real issue by directing attention from Saul's trouble to David's revelation, from the dramatic to the didactic. Browning, however, was unable to solve the problem by his own method when he published the first nine sections in 1845. When he returned to complete the poem in 1852, it would seem that he had come to accept Elizabeth Barrett's solution.

Clearly, the departure from his original intent was unfortunate, for it makes a convincing character study impossible. Browning was to learn that he had neither the sensibility nor the understanding to present the character of the primitive child-philosopher, and that his ability lay in treating the sophisticated, in developing conflicts growing out of opposing intellectual and emotional forces. Consequently, when he came to write *The Ring and the Book*, he made the Pope, not Pompilia, the spokesman of truth.

"Saul" is not successful, then, either as the development of a dramatic situation or of a consistent character. It was probably a sense of the poem's dramatic failure which caused Browning, after having classified it as a dramatic romance, to reclassify it first as a dramatic lyric, and finally as a lyric. This suggests a third possibility. If it is a successful lyric, we cannot quarrel because it is not something else. I should like now to examine the poem as a lyrical attempt to communicate a religious experience.

As such, the poem commends itself most readily. It has been called a mystical poem;[9] and this claim seems to have some support in the strong, almost hypnotic rhythm, the intense emotion, the symbolic suggestiveness of language, and the subordination of concept. The interpretation of the poem as a lyrical-mystical communication may be substantiated, however, only if matter and structure unite to present symbolically and perceptually the immediate sense of religious experience.

I contend that division of purpose and confusion of technique prevent the poem from being dramatic. The same dichotomy keeps it also from being successfully lyrical or mystical. Browning never completely reconciled the differences between parts written in 1845 and 1852. An even more serious disunity, however, is produced by the conflicts in both parts between the lyrical form and the sometimes lyrical, sometimes dramatic, sometimes argumentative matter.

Opposition between dramatic action and the ornate, lyrical structure is most painfully obvious in the first few stanzas. The structure thwarts the successful execution of the dramatic; and intrusion of the dramatic prevents a realization of the lyrical. The initial situation is inherently dramatic; but the needless repetition of word and phrase, the highly pictorial, Pre-Raphaelite description and imagery, the overpowering rhythm, and the radical inversion of syntax serve only to impede action and create a sense of divided purpose. Particularly distracting is the opposition created by the elaborate rhymes or near rhymes within the line, used apparently for decorative purposes:

> ". . . Ere I *tell*, ere thou *speak*,
> "Kiss my *cheek*, wish me *well!*" Then I wished it,
>   and did kiss his *cheek*.

> And *ran* o'er the *sand* burnt to powder.

> Far away from his *kind*, in the *pine*, till
>   deliverance come
> With the spring-*time*.

The practice of decorative rhyming suggests again the influence of Elizabeth Barrett. These lines illustrate the generally tenuous relationship in "Saul" between matter and structure, either dramatic or lyrical.

In sections sixteen to eighteen Browning turns from a direct emotional and sensuous presentation to a reasoned defense of the Incarnation. These sections have been so often admired that they require special attention here. Their faulty psychology and dramatic ineffectiveness have already been discussed. They are scarcely more successful if the poem is considered as lyrical rather than dramatic, however, for they constitute a structural and material unit which is in the poem but not of the poem. I can illustrate their disrupting effect by analyzing sentence structure, imagery, diction.

In the earlier sections of the poem, the sentences are adequate for highly emotional, mystical expression, but are totally inappropriate for dramatic expression. They are long and frequently fragmentary, the syntax is often erratic, and there is a tremendous accumulation of adjective and adverb phrases. The loose structure, characterized by verbosity, numerous co-ordinate conjunctions, run-on lines, repetition of words and ideas, and orthographical ellipses and dashes, is held in shape by emotional and sensuous associations. There are no sharp distinctions to denote intellectual firmness. The ellipses, for example, used for an entirely different purpose in "The Bishop Orders His Tomb," serve here to eliminate pauses and to unite line after line, idea after idea by an unbroken, horizontally moving rhythm. These characteristics are appropriate for lyrical expression. But beginning with section sixteen, when David discards song for speech, the structure undergoes a change sufficiently radical to create a disjunctive effect. The sentences become shorter, the syntax more nearly normal, and the modifying elements less frequent. The rhetorical question replaces in importance the rhetorical exclamation, so frequent in the first fifteen sections. Obviously, the poet is struggling to unite matter and structure and is moving in the direction of conversational realism.

The rhythm, however, remains unchanged, although the pace is somewhat slowed by a more definite grouping of sentences into thought groups; by omission of some of the co-ordinates, the dashes, the ellipses; and by more definite breaks in the rhythm. The cadences, too, become slightly more colloquial. There remains a plethora of words beyond those necessary to convey the argument directly and convincingly. In fact, both rhythm and copiousness of expression are irreconcilably opposed to the argumentative matter and to the effort toward greater colloquial realism. The result is an artistic disunity destructive of lyrical expression.

A similar dichotomy is apparent in the imagery. In the earlier stanzas it has a lush, pictorial quality which helps explain Dante Gabriel Rossetti's admiration for the younger Browning:

> . . . God's child with his dew
> On thy gracious gold hair, and those lilies
>   still living and blue
> Just broken to twine round thy harp-strings. . . .

One suspects that the word *gracious* was inserted only because the rhythm demanded the extra syllables, and because the word contained long vowels and alliterated with *gold*.[10] In sections nine and nineteen imagery is used as a medium for expressing a psychological state of mind. It becomes functional in the poem, communicating in the ninth section primarily the joys of this life, and in the nineteenth the awesome sense of God's presence in creation both as law and as love. It is characterized chiefly by animation and gains its effects largely by cumulative impact, as the concluding lines of the poem illustrate:

> E'en the serpent that slid away silent,—he felt
>   the new law.

The same stared in the white humid faces upturned
    by the flowers;
The same worked in the heart of the cedar and
    moved the vine-bowers:
And the little brooks witnessing murmured, persistent
    and low,
With their obstinate, all but hushed voices—
    "E'en so, it is so!"

The imagery in sections sixteen to eighteen, however, has neither the lushness of the first nor the alive-
ness of the later. It is colorless, passive, conceptual: "the
whole round of creation," "has gained an abyss, where
a dew-drop was asked," "life's dayspring, death's minute
of night," "the gates of new life." A relationship exists
between image and matter in both sections nine and nineteen and sections sixteen through eighteen, but no way
is provided for bringing them all together in a satisfying
relationship.

In the diction also there is division. In the first nine
sections, the substantives are concrete, those most often
used being *tent, hand, man,* and *head.* The modifiers too
are dominantly sensuous and perceptual. When Browning decided to complete the poem in 1852, he took to the
task a different vocabulary, consisting primarily of abstract nouns and qualitative and quantitative modifiers.
The shift of emphasis from the perceptual to the conceptual is obvious. Although many of the nouns are romantic and atmospheric, the modifiers are strictly evaluative: *new, right, perfect, good, great, almighty, whole.*
Here, then, as in the sentence structure and the imagery,
we find the same disunity between the earlier and latter

sections, between sections sixteen through eighteen and the rest of the poem.

I earlier designated Browning's characteristic unity as a tension between disparities. "Saul" abounds in disparities, material and structural, but is deficient in effective unifying devices, although rhythm, repetition, and symbol are intended to serve this function.

The most impelling feature of the poem is its rhythm. The generally smooth anapaestic movement reflects as much the influence of Elizabeth Barrett as any other element in the poem.[11] "Saul" is one of Browning's few poems which may be called musical. Wellek has remarked:

With such romantic poets as Tieck and, later, Verlaine, the attempts to achieve musical effects are largely attempts to suppress the meaning structure of verse, to avoid logical constructions, to stress connotations rather than denotations.[12]

Rhythm functions in "Saul" precisely as described here. In the first nine stanzas the "wild joys of living" and in the last the almost ineffable exaltation of religious communion are expressed in a strongly accentuated, rapidly moving rhythm:

I know not too well how I found my way home in
    the night.
There were witnesses, cohorts about me, to left and
    to right,
Angels, powers, the unuttered, unseen, the alive,
    the aware:

. . .

. . . The whole earth was awakened,
   hell loosed with her crews;
And the stars of night beat with emotion, and tingled
   and shot
Out in fire the strong pain of pent knowledge.

Here and in other sections where denotation is unimportant, the effect in general is what it should be.

Even in these, however, there are disturbing imperfections. The basic anapaestic pattern is so forcefully established that the kind of shifting stress found in most of Browning's poems becomes distracting in this one. In one sense the overwhelming strength of rhythm and its triumph over idea are appropriate in a poem regarded by some critics as mystical. On the other hand, there are obvious deviations from the basic pattern which serve no material or structural purpose. In many lines no satisfactory reconciliation can be effected between meaning and rhythm. A few obvious examples from "Saul" are:

With the spring-time—so agonized Saul, drear and stark,
   blind and dumb,

Then I tuned my harp,—took off the lilies we twine
   round its cords,

Grasps at hand, eye lights eye in good fellowship,
   and great hearts expand,

So the head: but the body still moved not, still
   hung there erect,

Such result as, from seething grape-bundles, the spirit
   strained true.

The trouble in these is that the ultimate effect is not a triumph of emotion and sense over mind as we find it in many of Shelley's, Tennyson's, and Swinburne's poems, and as it well might be in "Saul," but an uncomfortable compromise between emotional expression and colloquial realism. No artistic purpose is served by ruggedness in a poem where the desired communion is complete. In "Two in the Campagna," on the other hand, where perfect understanding and union are frustrated, the broken rhythm is symbolically expressive. Although these occasional imperfections exist, and must be accounted artistic flaws, the rhythmic pattern is generally appropriate in highly emotional, perceptive passages. But its ineffectiveness in the earlier, more dramatic sections has already been noticed. Further, in sections sixteen to eighteen, it is equally unsuccessful since it hinders a clear, forceful expression of idea, which appears to be the poet's objective. In spite of the slightly more colloquial cadence and the abandonment of devices which blend lines into emotional and sensuous rather than conceptual units, the opposition between matter and structure is not satisfactorily reconciled. The difference is so fundamental that even the powerful rhythmic pattern fails to acomplish the desired unity.

There are in the poem many kinds of repetition which should serve also as unifying devices. The rhyme pattern, unlike that of *Sordello* and "My Last Duchess," is pronounced. It functions structurally in that it helps define stanzaic form, but its chief purpose is to convey emotion and sensation, which it does by connotation rather than denotation. It is the total effect of the pattern, not the specific effects growing out of the parts, that is impressive. Elements fail to unite to form either conceptual or atmospheric groups. There are, for example, one hundred and sixty-four rhyming units (composed of from two to four words each) and in only two is there repetition. Nor can any group from among the total number be formed of associated words which convey particular conceptual or emotional meanings. Rhyme actually serves to subdue thought and to stimulate emotion and sensation, but, like rhythm, it functions in opposition to meaning both in the early dramatic portion of the poem and in sections sixteen through eighteen.

Less repetition of key words and more repetition of phrase and structure are found in "Saul" than in any other poem included in this study. The noun *life* and the adjective *new* are the only words repeated noticeably, but there is constant repetition of phrase and structural feature: "Ere I tell, ere thou speak," "with the honey be bright, with the water be wet," ". . . of prayer nor of praise," ". . . drear and stark, blind and dumb," "All the heart and the soul and the senses . . . ," "by man and by brute . . . ," "Thy whole people, the countless. . . ." The chief purpose of this repetition is to maintain rhythmic pattern and to create pleasantness of sound; in short, it is connotative and perceptual. Repetition of vowels and consonants, of which there is a great deal, serves the same end. Although recurrence of words, phrases, structural features, vowels, and consonants performs a kind of unifying function, it is unsuccessful artistically because insufficiently comprehensive to render the poem coherent.

A third device which works ostensibly for unity is a symbolism, suggestive, however, rather than satisfyingly communicative. *Light-darkness* and *wine*, correlatives of *new* and *life*, appear to have symbolic meaning, yet it is difficult to determine of what, precisely, they are symbolic. They are terms strong with Christian associations, and in a poem treating the Incarnation they might be expected to have traditional symbolic value. *Light-darkness* probably does have. Saul is in darkness; his spiritual state is a blackness; a sunray, signaling the coming of Christ and the new life, dramatically penetrates the darkness. Finally, the poem concludes with the dawning of a new day and the rebirth of all creation.

In the broad outline the intent of the light-darkness symbol is clear and functions to emphasize the central meaning of the poem. It even serves partly to communicate directly a sense of religious communion. Yet the effect lacks sharpness, because both *light* and *darkness* are also used figuratively in manners not related to the main symbol:

> Lest they snap 'neath the stress of the noontide—
> those sunbeams like swords!

> And now one after one seeks its lodging, as star
> follows star,

> . . . each bidding rejoice
> Saul's fame in the light it was made for—

> I looked up and dared gaze at those eyes, nor was
> hurt any more
> Than by slow pallid sunsets in autumn. . . .

Here lack of focus and control creates intellectual and emotional diffusion. Browning's artistry is carefully exercised, on the other hand, in his better works such as "Andrea del Sarto," in which symbol becomes one of the major unifying devices.

The wine symbol is even more elusive. In a poem dealing with the Incarnation but ignoring the Atonement, precision cannot, perhaps, be expected. Initially, wine symbolizes sentient and physical life, the "wild joys of living"; later it acquires additional meaning:

> His cup with the wine of this life, pressing
> all that it yields
> Of mere fruitage, the strength and the beauty:
> beyond on what fields,
> Glean a vintage more potent and perfect to
> brighten the eye
> And bring blood to the lip, and commend them
> the cup they put by?

In the latter part of the poem it comes to be symbolic of a vague "spirituality" which may mean either life of the mind as opposed to life of the senses, or simply an influence, a kind of immortality, that projects itself into future generations. It is, indeed, suggested somewhat uncertainly that it symbolizes eternal life. David speaks once of wine as the final product of the cultivated vine, a symbol of something man is to strive for; again he refers to it as a drink capable of enlarging man's vision, of providing him with the eyes of the "seer."

In both cases, however, the symbol is imprecise and the intent uncertain. Vagueness of concept and expression prohibits symbolism from serving as an effective instrument of communication. This becomes a serious criticism because at least a portion of the poem is given to theological argumentation, which must be precise, not merely suggestive.

Nor is the love analogy entirely clear. David's human love for Saul, his willingness to sacrifice himself, suggests that there must be a greater divine love; what David as man desires for Saul, God must surely provide in time —hence the inevitable Incarnation (the rationality of this argument is foreign to the spirit of the Psalms). David thus becomes the prototype of God, but Saul has already been symbolically cast in the role of Christ. The precise relationship between the two figures becomes confusing.

Neither alone, nor compositely, do rhythm, repetition, or symbol succeed in overcoming the discordant elements and in making of the recalcitrant matter an artistic whole. The poem fails as an expression of lyrical, mystic expression, just as it failed as drama, because all sections are never poetically assimilated. Although Elizabeth Barrett contributed in many ways to Browning's general development, it would seem that her influence in this poem was not entirely wholesome.

The poem is not characteristic of Browning's best work and, by contrast, serves to point up the qualities upon which the poet's future reputation will most surely depend. As a dramatic poem it lacks unity of action, psychological penetration, colloquial realism, and, most important, the peculiar kind of intellectual and emotional complexity and disparity out of which Browning creates his distinctive unity. The poem does not succeed as a lyric, although Browning was capable of writing successful lyrics, because it lacks intellectual and artistic centrality, material and structural unity. It demonstrates also how when Browning failed as an artist his poetry could degenerate into didacticism, depending for its effects upon stock responses to trite sentiment and moral aphorisms.

One word more. "Saul" illustrates also that, although Browning was fascinated by the idea of the "infinite moment" and the "one experience," he was rarely able to communicate it effectively. He treats the subject in numerous love poems and in "Karshish" and "The Two Poets of Croisic"; and part of his admiration for Christopher Smart resulted from his erroneous belief that Smart produced only one fine poem, "A Song to David," and that in a fit of madness. He could not have known *Rejoice in the Lamb*, the manuscript of which was not discovered until 1939. If "Saul" were influenced by Smart, as DeVane thinks, it is not surprising that Browning should want to communicate David's one, ultimate, and all revealing moment:

> Then the truth came upon me. No harp more—
> no song more!

But in spite of his elaborate and partly effective technique, he failed to present the experience itself symbolically and perceptually. Like Donne, he talks poetically about mystical and religious experience, but is unable to communicate a sense of the experience itself. Although Donne fails to write mystical poetry, he triumphs on another level. Projecting the whole of himself into his work—both his impulse toward multiplicity and his desire for singleness of purpose and devotion—he creates a poetry out of conflict:

Oh, to vex me, contraryes meet in one:
Inconstancy unnaturally hath begott
A constant habit; that when I would not
I change in vowes, and in devotione.

                    . . . for I
Except you'enthrall mee, never shall be free,
Nor ever chast, except you ravish mee.

In "Saul" we feel that something less than the whole
Browning is present. The poet fails to hold simultaneously and steadfastly to the whole of his experience,
intellectual and emotional. A vague emotionalism without intellectual precision and intensity produces neither
mystical synthesis, nor dramatic tension; neither the
quality of Dante's *Divine Comedy*, on the one hand, nor
of Donne's *Holy Sonnets*, "Riding Westward," "Hymne
to God my God, in My Sicknesse," or of Browning's
own "Bishop Blougram's Apology," on the other.

Part of Browning's usual success comes from a realization of his abilities and the choice of materials and
structure appropriate for that which he can best do. But
in "Saul" Browning's objective is not single and his
structure is not uniformly appropriate. As a result, "Saul"
is brilliant in parts but lacks artistic wholeness.

The Bow and
the Lyre

I

Certain recurrent material and structural practices in "Andrea del Sarto," "Fra Lippo Lippi," "The Bishop Orders His Tomb," and "Bishop Blougram's Apology" suggest themselves as characterizing Browning's art, a conclusion strengthened by the fact that their absence in "Saul" partly explains its ineffectiveness.

It might be argued that five poems are an insufficient number upon which to generalize; it can scarcely be held, however, that the technique which produced four of Browning's best poems is insignificant. I shall describe this technique, and at the same time suggest tentatively that it also characterizes the larger body of Browning's shorter poems.

Two things are important about Browning's matter. First, the kind to which he is attracted: what in general distinguishes his characters, situations, ideas, and emotions? Second, the nature and mode of his seeing, his "vision" of life: what intellectual and emotional vortex provides the organizing center of his artistic perspective?

It is not enough to enumerate the possible sources from which he gathered material, or to catalogue the situations and characters which he developed, though both have been done with considerable energy. It is more relevant to observe that Browning's choice of material was dictated by a principle which both indicates his personal sympathies and helps explain the quality and texture of his work: his interest in situation and character in which there are conflicts, incongruities, and paradox.

Although all poets write of conflicts, Browning's are individual and may be described as a distinctive characteristic of his work. Browning wrote dramatic poetry and is generally conceded to have contributed more than any other poet to the development of the monologue, yet his conflicts are infrequently situational. He explained clearly his failure to write for the stage when he said that his ability was to portray action in character rather than character in action. There are movement and development in "Fra Lippo Lippi," "Andrea del Sarto," "The Bishop Orders His Tomb," and "Bishop Blougram's Apology," although all are too static situationally for the stage. The poems are dramatic because of the conflicts and resolutions or compromises within the characters. Rightly, again, Browning indicated his real strength when he asserted that in *Sordello* his "stress lay on the incidents in the development of a soul: little else is worth study."

Even in the narrative poems, conflict is more internal than external, as, for example, it is in "Iv̀an Iv̀anovitch," "Halbert and Hob," and "A Forgiveness." All these poems, in contrast to "Saul," are genuinely dramatic.

Browning's lack of interest in story as story is suggested by *The Ring and the Book*, in which he violates traditional narrative principles by relating the same events over and over, each time for the purpose of exploring a new level of meaning as it is shaped by a different consciousness.

Always psychological in effect, the conflict is sometimes within the character, sometimes between the character and the external world, sometimes between the character and forces perhaps neither of his own nor his world's making. Andrea's conflicts are between the real and the ideal, Lippo's between body and soul, the Bishop of St. Praxed's between what he had imagined himself and what by death he was proved to be, Bishop Blougram's between an instinctive need for God and a skeptical and disbelieving mind. Because Browning is sensitive of differences among his characters, these typical conflicts, appearing throughout his poetry, manifest themselves in different degrees of intensity and produce diverse ends.

Often the conflict is between two points of view and the poem is argumentative. More often than not the argument, ostensibly between two characters, is actually between diverse forces within the speaker. Browning's characters are frequently, like Oedipus, both hero and villain, but unlike Oedipus they rarely achieve genuine self-discovery, purgation. Browning's mode is ironic, not tragic. In the better of his argumentative poems, "Bishop Blougram's Apology," for example, Browning recognizes complexities, describing the mind in the process of formulating ideas, establishing a relationship between thought, feeling, and sense. Ideas become not ends in themselves but stimuli for the total experience incarnate in structure.

Of course, Browning is not always successful. In "Saul," "A Death in the Desert," and "Rabbi Ben Ezra," for example, he compromises with Victorian expectations that poets perform explicitly as prophets, establishing himself on what he thought to be Pisgah but which in reality was only the Browning Society. In these poems, where ideas remain poetically passive, there are little development of character, almost no conflict, and insufficient emotional and sensuous realization of idea. Also, Browning's argumentative poems are sometimes marred by lack of detachment. In "Mr. Sludge, 'The Medium,' " for example, Browning fails to maintain artistic distance and to create realistic conflict. The reader never feels that Mr. Sludge may be partly right, and what might have been a convincing psychological poem remains an invective. On the other hand, although "Bishop Blougram's Apology" reflects contemporary interests and treats a subject on which Browning had strong personal feelings, it demonstrates remarkably his ability to write objectively and poetically.

Sometimes the conflict is against incomprehensible, intangible forces that flaw man's nature or creation itself. Andrea is the victim of an inner emptiness not entirely of his own making; the lovers in "Two in the Compagna" are thwarted by forces beyond their comprehension; Martin Relph's silence is involuntary, not deliberate. In much of Browning's poetry, there is a sense of man's impotence in the presence of evil, of fate:

Just when I seemed about to learn!
Where is the thread now? Off again!
The old trick! Only I discern—
    Infinite passion, and the pain
    Of finite hearts that yearn.

Browning's sense of conflict expresses itself partly through recurring incongruities in his poetry—the spider in the communion cup, the toad in the christening font. No poet has insisted more strenuously than Browning on the complexity of human motives, the illusion of appearances, on ambiguity. In "Gold Hair," for example, he exposes the miserliness of a young girl commonly regarded as a saint. Both the Bishop of St. Praxed's and Gigadibs are deceived by appearances and their drama is one of gradual self-revelation. Lippo, so ostentatiously sensuous, displays, with apparent contradiction, a sensitivity to beauty and spirit. From the time Browning created Pippa's "happiest four" to the end of his career, he had a fondness for exposing the goodness of the scoundrel (*Fifine at the Fair, Prince Hohenstiel-Schwangau*) and the weakness of the idealized ("Count Gismond," "Clive.") Browning's own consciousness appears divided by a dialectic which finds full expression only in contradictory symbols: the spider in the communion cup, the toad in the christening font.

Browning proposes to create a unified poem and at the same time retain inviolate its elements of conflict. His aim is not to cancel out and de-intensify, but to relate counterforces so as to create a new level of meaning. Abt Vogler implies what seems also to be Browning's aesthetic theory:

And I know not if, save in this, such gift be
   allowed to man,
That out of three sounds he frame, not a fourth
   sound, but a star.

It is characteristic that the unity, the balance which
Browning creates is a tenuous one: in the Bishop's words,
that of a tightrope walker.

I am at present concerned with the effect of this
ambivalency upon Browning's choice of material. That
he was an optimist has often been dogmatically maintained, yet few of his characters attain unfailing serenity.
Probable exceptions are Pippa and, possibly, Abt Vogler
and Rabbi Ben Ezra. But Pippa's serenity is based upon
childish innocence, and her often quoted affirmation is
juxtaposed against contradictory evils. Abt Vogler is
fully aware of the "broken arcs," and both he and the
Rabbi accept earth's roughness as part of the divine plan
whereby man is prepared for a better life. Nowhere does
Browning express hope that this life can be made materially better. Although certain of his characters profess
the worthwhileness of effort, none realizes utopian
dreams. For the most part, Browning's men and women
are confused, disturbed, tortured: Sordello, Paracelsus,
Pictor Ignotus, Instans Tyrannus, Porphyria's Lover,
Childe Roland, Jacques du Bourg-Molay, Mr. Sludge,
Pacchiarotto, Léonce Miranda, to name only a few.

In his earlier poems, he sometimes attempted to resolve tensions and to achieve a romantic synthesis. The
apocalyptic vision of Paracelsus, for example, appears as
a *deus ex machina* designed to give the poem what the
youthful poet, strongly influenced by the Romantics, felt

should be its proper conclusion. Actually, it prevented a clearer realization of that quality which distinguishes his mature work. In his later poems he de-emphasized the deathbed revelation, the capsuling of all Truth into one momentary vision, and set himself to treat dramatically the intellectual, emotional, sensuous impact of conflicts upon his dramatis personae.

It is noteworthy that Browning's characters so often fail, and, as I have suggested, for reasons not of their own making. Some, like Sordello, are genuinely confused and cannot make important decisions; some, like Paracelsus, make sincere but wrong choices; others, Andrea perhaps, are prevented by the "old trick" from making a choice at all; and still others fail to act even though they know partly what they should do. Neither Andrea, Fra Lippo, or the Bishop of St. Praxed's achieves integration; Bishop Blougram is left unsatisfied by what appears his more successful attempt; David has his vision, but the structure of the poem is distorted through its presentation.

It must be emphasized, too, that many among Browning's characters fail for reasons other than the "ungirt loin" and the "unlit lamp" (phrases which used out of context have often led to flagrant oversimplification). There is much wrong in Browning's imaginative world that action will not cure. It is ironic that Andrea suffers from inactivity on the one hand, but would only have been more thoroughly damned by action, on the other. The lovers in "The Statue and the Bust" might have absolved themselves on one level if they had acted, but at the same time would have incurred on another level an additional guilt, as Browning clearly implies. To find Browning's "philosophy" in this one poem is to find it partly. There are in Browning many levels of damnation—and as many salvations.

Browning's attraction to both conflict and failure is illustrated in his love poems. His own romance has been so sentimentalized that one expects his lovers to be happy and successful; yet they are most often frustrated. Andrea, Fra Lippo, and the Bishop of St. Praxed's are all thwarted, unhappy lovers. Some fail because they do not take opportunity when it presents itself: "Dîs aliter visum," "Too Late," "Youth and Art"; some because love ends in boredom, misunderstanding, estrangement, or betrayal: "A Woman's Last Word," "Misconception," "In a Year," "The Confessional," "A Lover's Quarrel," "Any Wife to Any Husband." Even the idealized love of Pompilia and Caponsacchi ends tragically. And surely one of Browning's most poignant poems is "Two in the Compagna," which tells of barriers between two lovers which won't be broken down. These conflict-producing situations stimulate reactions ranging from the quiet hopelessness of the speaker in "Two in the Compagna" to the pathological violence of "Porphyria's Lover."

Browning's characters, often tormented by incomprehensible forces, are frequently frustrated, neurotic. For example, in "Evelyn Hope," "Porphyria's Lover," "Cristina," he treats the abnormal lover; in "Johannes Agricola in Meditation" and Red Cotton Night-Cap Country, the religious fanatic.

In his choice of subject matter, then, Browning demonstrates intellectual and psychological consistency.

The characteristics which I have described—interest in conflict, incongruity, failure, and abnormality—are differing expressions of a unified sensibility.

Complementary to this subject matter is Browning's skeptical attitude and dramatic technique. Materials of frustration, innately chaotic, are given pattern and meaning by a particular mode of "seeing" which is at once a part of the frustration and its organizing center. Browning's was a skeptical mind rendering him temperamentally unfit to write strongly in the first person "R. B., A Poem." (Witness "Saul.") Throughout his career he maintained that his poems were impersonal, and toward the end of his life he impatiently insisted on keeping separate the man and the poet ("The House," "At the 'Mermaid' "). He appears suspicious of dogmatic formulations. Without judging the relative merits of the objective and the subjective poet, distinctions in which he displayed interest in his essay on Shelley, it is enough to note here that his preference for the dramatic gave to his best works their peculiar texture. His notable effects come not from the sudden, synthesized "Epiphany," but from the dramatic interplay between differing modes of seeing and feeling.

Browning was not satisfied with narrow perspectives and dogmatic statements. Unwilling to fix permanently upon one "truth," he avoided the single point of view, preferring rather to approach problems from different intellectual and emotional positions, juxtaposing one against the other, holding in suspension a personal commitment to either. Hence the dramatis personae: Andrea and Fra Lippo, David and Bishop Blougram.

Through his different men and women he was able to give expression to many possible views.

Browning's, then, was a multiple vision inclusive of differing modes of expression. Both his materials of frustration and his skeptical attitude are suggested by many titles which express duality: *Bells and Pomegranates, Jocoseria, Tufts and Towers*. He habitually placed pairs of poems or sections of poems in dialectical juxtaposition: "Meeting at Night"—"Parting at Morning"; "By the Fireside"—"Any Wife to Any Husband" (placed side by side in the first edition of *Men and Women*); "One Way of Love"—"Another Way of Love"; "Before"—"After." Conflicting points of view are expressed in different poems: "A Grammarian's Funeral"—"Sibrandus Schafnaburgensis"; "Pisgah-Sights, I-II"—"Prospice"; "Fear and Scruples"—"Saul"; "Numpholeptos"—"Epilogue to Asolando."

It is impossible to say on the basis of any one poem that Browning believed this or that about God or life. Andrea presents one view of art, Lippo another; David one position on religion, Bishop Blougram another. Though all Browning had to say about either art or religion is no doubt self-revelatory (as is the fact also that he avoided speaking in his own person), nothing less than the whole can be taken as even approaching his thoughts.

Browning's oblique dramatic method, suggested by the poems treated here, is implicit in *The Ring and the Book*. The poet had before him a set of facts representing something less than "truth," which he recognized as complex and elusive. Consequently, in his poem several observers, none all right or all wrong, present their stories from their own points of view. Thus, Browning explores every facet of the affair before introducing the Pope, representative of the highest spiritual and intellectual development of his time, to speak finally upon the matter. Even the Pope assumes the role of judge with hesitancy, prefacing his judgment with a questioning discussion of papal infallibility. Certainty was difficult for both the Pope and Browning. In his better work, Browning is the objective observer of life, hesitating to make statements, preferring always to speak through characters who may or may not express the poet's own view, or who express it but partially or hypothetically. He is unwilling to trust the responsibility of saying everything to any one person, even to himself.

Browning's poetry, then, may be read on two levels: each poem may be read as an entity or in the context of Browning's whole work. The better poems contain within themselves all the parts essential to their total meaning, making it unnecessary for the critic to go outside the poem for his interpretation. Although neither Andrea, nor Lippo, nor Bishop Blougram speaks for Browning, each is fully conceived and a logical part of the imaginative world in which he is placed. That "Saul" must be read partly in light of the conditions under which it was written seems to me a defect.

We see more clearly the complexity of the poet's thinking about art, for example, if when we read "Andrea del Sarto" we remember also "Fra Lippo Lippi," "Abt Vogler," "Pictor Ignotus," and "How It Strikes a Contemporary." If Browning failed to write a successful stage play, he did succeed in creating a repertory of characters, who, appearing in separate poems, still have a dynamic relationship with each other. And, although we may enjoy the single poem without establishing this relationship, we appreciate more the scope and depth of Browning's achievement when we do. Empson's statement about dramatic irony may be applied to Browning's work:

Also the device sets your judgment free because you need not identify yourself firmly with any one of the characters . . . ; a situation is repeated for quite different characters, and this puts the main interest in the situation not the character. Thus the effect of having two old men with ungrateful children, of different sorts, is to make us generalize the theme of Lear and feel that whole classes of children have become unfaithful, all nature is breaking up, as in the storm. The situation is made something valuable in itself, perhaps for reasons hardly realized; it can work on you like a myth.[1]

How specifically does this relate to Browning's technique? His repeated treatment of situation from different points of view serves a purpose similar to that described by Empson. It eliminates didacticism and narrowness from his better poems because the reader is not required to identify himself permanently with any one character; it diverts his attention from the immediate and particular to the recurring and the general; it transforms the individual into the universal, giving scope and magnitude to what Browning has to say about any subject.

Browning's multiple vision (implicit in his choice of materials, his skeptical attitude, and his objective technique) increases the potentiality of his work for stimulating aesthetic response. It is well, at the outset, to recognize some of his limitations. He rarely attains the tragic vision; he does not succeed in creating the serene character; he is unable to communicate religious truth mystically ("Saul," for example). It might be said that he descends with Dante into hell, achieves purgatory, but never quite attains paradise.

When these shortcomings are acknowledged, however, there is yet much to justify calling him a major poet. In his work there is range, depth, intensity, irony, paradox, wit, whimsy, and humor. He grasped sympathetically and penetratingly numerous points of view extending from skepticism ("Fear and Scruples") to cautious affirmation ("Fra Lippo Lippi"). His characters range in complexity from the naïve simplicity of Pippa to the sophisticated subtlety of Bishop Blougram. He treats love as mere lust in Ottima; and in Pompilia, although he never achieves the etherealized vision of Dante's Beatrice, he approaches it. The objectivity, hence the honesty, with which he dramatizes ideas and emotions within his scope, gives him breadth of appeal and provides a vision of life that should remain meaningful. It would be difficult to find in the nineteenth century a more comprehensive and penetrating poet.

His mode of seeing gives his work intensity. The counterbalancing of opposing forces plays one against another, increasing the vividness, hence the poetic effectiveness, of both. The juxtaposition in "Andrea del Sarto" of the real and the ideal, of the desire and the impotency, gives poignancy to the poem. In both "Fra Lippo Lippi" and "Bishop Blougram's Apology" intellectual and emotional intensity of another kind is achieved. Browning's intensity is primarily intellectual and emotional, certainly not "muscular," as is sometimes maintained.

In his middle period he generally sustained the tension; in his latter he too often sacrificed it. Apparently, he grew weary of struggling with oppositions, of trying to focus his vision. He became less willing to suspend judgment, more inclined to assert himself, yielding more and more to the "prophetic" urge, latent in some of his earlier work, ostentatious in "Saul."

Ferishtah's Fancies (1884), one of his weakest volumes, illustrates my point. Like "Saul" it treats no genuine conflict, hence it lacks intellectual and emotional vividness. Ferishtah prosaically expounds a "philosophy." But even here, Browning does not surrender completely his skepticism, and in the epilogue, speaking in his own person, he provides one of his most effective ironies. Against Ferishtah's confidence he juxtaposes his own uncertainty:

> Only, at heart's utmost joy and triumph, terror
> Sudden turns the blood to ice: a chill
>   wind disencharms
> All the late enchantment! What if all be error—
> If the halo irised round my head were, Love,
>   thine arms?

Browning is inevitably the poet of paradox and irony. The deceptiveness of appearances; the co-existence, even the dual nature, of good and evil, beauty and ugliness; man's proclivity for self-deception and his inability to disentangle and order the diversities produced by life's paradoxes make the poet an ironist on a cosmic scale. In this respect, more than any other, he is un-Romantic. His vision lacks the intense concentration, the single faith, the optimistic belief in social ameliora-tion characteristic of the Romantics. He is content to treat the problem tentatively and skeptically, to con-centrate upon its psychological impact upon character; the Romantics sought the solution and described the ecstasy of discovery. Browning's poetry of "violently yoked" opposites aligns him with the Baroque writers of the seventeenth century and makes him also a forerunner of twentieth-century poets.

One final observation. Browning's way of seeing produces the distinctive quality of his humor. Though it is inaccurate to say that nineteenth-century poets lacked a sense of humor, certainly, in general, they distinguished sharply between humor and "high seriousness." But Browning used humor seriously in serious poetry. One should not be deceived if he detects in some of his work what John Ciardi calls the "cathedral atmosphere," for in Browning's cathedral there may be spiders in the com-munion cup and toads in the christening font. It is not always clear whether they are supposed to provoke laughter or tears. But if they are practical jokes they are grim ones.

2

Browning was often called obscure, indeed, some-times wilfully obscure, by his Victorian critics. Their charge of wilfulness often seems ill-tempered; that of ob-scurity, imperceptive. His apparent difficulty arises only indirectly from his profundity, his dialectical and psychological subtleties; directly from his structure, which he intended to be an embodiment, an externalization of matter.

As the ultimate form of expression, structure is implicit in matter, taking its shape from those characteristics which I have just described. As a stock of devices, it is an active, shaping, inseparable part of meaning itself. Juxtaposition, irony, and paradox are at once structural and material; diction, sentence structure, repetition, rhythm, and imagery both produce and are produced by meaning. Even punctuation and ellipses are organic. In a poem so conversational as "The Bishop Orders His Tomb," for example, much of the meaning is carried in orthographical symbols suggesting attitude, tone, and thought not communicable through words alone. In Browning's monologues these devices serve much the same purpose as stage directions in a play, and at the same time remind us how different the monologue is from a play.

His style, a proper approach to meaning, can neither be explained as the product of literary influences, nor be satisfactorily analyzed by externally applied linguistic methods. Its character is ontological; it is co-existent with matter; both unite to express the "poem."

Browning may be said to have two styles: the specific and the general. The one individualizes the separate monologue; the other, stimulated by his interest and his mode of seeing, characterizes his work as a whole. Of the former I have already spoken; of the latter primarily I wish now to speak. His structure is a precise expression of clearly formulated ideas and emotions; his poems are dramatic, presenting a fully developed speaker compelled to communicate to a listener (more adequately developed in some cases than in others); the tone, structure, and cadence are colloquial; the unity is a tension produced by the interplay of opposing intellectual and emotional forces.

His precision is noticed first in his language, an important contribution to English poetry. Most literary reforms first express themselves structurally in a revitalized diction. Once the initial impulse of a literary movement loses its imaginative grip upon poets, language gets separated from meaning and becomes "poetic"—stereotyped and uncommunicative. When this happens, it is time for a rethinking, a reunion of matter and structure. English literary history is a record of disintegration and reconstruction; its important figures are the poets able to re-establish or to maintain the poem as a unified expression. Inevitably the poetic reformer creates a new language. Eliot has discussed Donne's, Dryden's, and Wordsworth's contributions to the modes of literary expression associated with their names.[2] As Pound and Ford have pointed out, Browning also was a precursor, for in his use of words and in the theory it implied, he pointed toward the "new" poetry of the twentieth century. Different as these four men are in many ways, they share the great poets' sensitiveness to the organic nature of the poem.

Browning's work is remarkably free of "poetic" language, either neo-classical or romantic. His passion for precision and his multiple awareness brought into poetry an extensive and polyglot language which may suggest superficially a lack of discrimination. In "Fra Lippo Lippi," for example, there are learned, poetic, archaic, unfamiliar, colloquial, and slang words. But—and this is the important point—they all have functional purposes.

It has been suggested to imply prosaicness that once Browning determined to become a poet, he initiated his preparation by reading the whole of Johnson's dictionary.[3] Later, he became also a close student of the *Oxford English Dictionary*. It is not precisely clear to me, however, why this interest in language should indicate unpoetic imagination. I should say, rather, that his precise knowledge of words provided the medium for expressing accurately his meanings. Actually, Browning used a distinctive diction for each of his better poems. In "Fra Lippo Lippi" there are forty words that occur nowhere else in Browning's poetry. As a rule, it is safer to generalize about Lippo's, Andrea's, or Bishop Blougram's diction than about Browning's.

He avoided the romantic connotative use of words. The language of "Andrea del Sarto," "Fra Lippo Lippi," "The Bishop Orders His Tomb," and "Bishop Blougram's Apology," precise and denotative, is always concerned to establish a particular character in a particular situation. When it is not so employed, the poem generally fails for other reasons also. In "Saul," for example, where character and situation are inadequately defined, connotative language is accompanied by vaguely suggestive, imprecise thoughts and emotions, and loose organization. Customarily, however, Browning does not use words for cumulative emotional effects; his repetitions are intended primarily to accentuate idea or to enforce symbolic meaning. His poetry, in general, lacks modifiers and other words used merely to decorate or to fill out rhythm patterns. What at first may appear copiousness proves to be something quite different. In "Fra Lippo Lippi" and "Bishop Blougram's Apology," expansiveness reflects active minds, not satisfied with direct statements, but intent upon exploring every detail of a complex matter. Browning's better monologues do not suffer from a plethora of words, as Whitman's poems do, because for Browning's words there are intellectual and emotional equivalents.

The precise relation between language and meaning may be illustrated by noting how appropriately language expresses his diverse way of seeing. In "Andrea del Sarto," it functions symbolically to dramatize the conflicts between Andrea's ideal and the reality; in "Fra Lippo Lippi," to present counteracting forces in the monk-artist's personality. In the latter the connotative instability of abstract and concrete words suggests the reconciliation which Lippo sought between his two worlds. Browning, in contrast to most nineteenth-century poets, introduces the pun into serious poetry because it provides concise expression of ambivalency.

Additionally, and for much the same purpose, he uses numerous compounds, particularly apparent in "Fra Lippo Lippi." According to Massey, there are in his work over twice as many (more than three thousand) as in Keats' and Shelley's poetry combined.[4] Approximately half of these are original, the others being taken primarily from Greek and Elizabethan literature. In contrast to Shelley, who uses in combination such words as *wind*, *lightning*, *mountain*, *cloud*, and *star*, and to Keats, who compounds primarily sound and color words, Browning is drawn towards the qualitative and quantitative combinations: *self-same*, *life-long*, *day-long*, being his favorite ones.

Browning's imagery, like his diction, is precise and organic. It lacks, probably for two reasons, both the intellectual subtlety of Donne's and the diffuse decorativeness of Shelley's. As Browning is less subjective than either Donne or Shelley, his imagery operates within stricter limitations. Further—and in this respect he is like Donne—he uses imagery as an integral part of a total expression. Because it is part of a pattern producing no effects independent of the whole, no "beauty" not inherent in the total meaning, his poetry, in contrast to that of Tennyson or Rossetti, seems particularly "unpoetic." The young lady, quoted by Oscar Wilde, who praised Browning for heading a reaction against beauty was probably more acute than she realized.

The precision of Browning's imagery is particularly noticeable in "Andrea del Sarto." Most of the images arise from a group of associated words—*worth, gold, gain, fame, reward*—which express the commercialism and perversion of his art and love. In "Fra Lippo Lippi" his juxtaposition within the image of the abstract and concrete expresses his conflict between spirit and sense. "The Bishop Orders His Tomb" appropriately lacks figurative complexity, for the image pattern must operate within the narrow limits of the Bishop's intellectual and emotional awareness.

Sometimes imagery functions symbolically. In "Andrea del Sarto," a contrast to "Saul," symbols are precise and controlled, serving to bring idea, emotion, and sensation into an expressive whole. In Lucrezia, the figures of commercialism, and the wall image, Browning finds expression for his complicated meaning. Characteristic of his diversity, he prefers metaphor, oxymoron, and paradox to simile, as I have demonstrated in my explication of the poems.

Single structural devices cannot be understood fully apart from others. A discussion of diction, imagery, and repetition, as illustrating Browning's precision, broadens to include sentence structure and rhythm, devices best discussed as single units. They demonstrate not only precision, but other features of Browning's style. They too have their origin in character and are shaped by certain conditions: the awareness of conflict, the desire to communicate a total experience, the compulsion to speak colloquially.

Browning's better poems do not give the impression of a pronouncement, but of a character thinking aloud, attempting to communicate to a listener. Fra Lippo must defend himself against the suspicions of the nightwatchman; the dying Bishop must persuade his sons to build a tomb; Bishop Blougram must answer Gigadibs' charges. Even Andrea, who speaks as much to himself as to Lucrezia, eschews the meaningless phrase, the decorative cadence.

The urgency to communicate derives partly from the fact that Browning presents his characters at climactic moments. Andrea, Fra Lippo, the Bishop of St. Praxed's, and Bishop Blougram—each is caught in an emotional and intellectual crisis. He has not time to formulate his thoughts but must defend himself extemporaneously. The characteristic Browning situation begins at an advanced stage and is often thrust upon the reader by an opening line that is colloquial both in syntax and cadence. Some representative first lines will illustrate: "Plague take all your pedants, say I!" "I am poor brother

Lippo, by your leave!" "It's a lie—their Priests, their Pope, / Their Saints . . . ," "My first thought was, he lied in every word," "But do not let us quarrel any more," "Stop playing, poet! May a brother speak?" "Stop, let me have the truth of that!" "Beautiful Evelyn Hope is dead," "Stand still, true poet that you are!"

This practice of introducing an already tense situation by a startling opening line is reminiscent of Donne: "For Godsake hold your tongue, and let me love," "Shee'is dead; and all which die / To their first Elements resolve," "Stand still, and I will read to thee / A Lecture," "Come, Madam, come, all rest my powers defie." (And Pound sometimes sounds like both Donne and Browning: "Hang it all, Robert Browning, there can be but one 'Sordello'!") Such dramatic beginnings establish the colloquial and dramatic mode of the entire poem.

Successful communication depends partly upon adequately developed speaker and listener, and the first criterion by which to judge a Browning monologue is the effectiveness of its characterization. "Andrea del Sarto" represents the consummation of Browning's art. In it both speaker and listener are sufficiently realized to produce, in their clash one with the other, the tension requisite for dramatic art.

Not all of Browning's auditors, however, serve as antagonist to stimulate conflict and initiate movement. In fact, this is not their primary function. Most often the central conflict of the poem is within the speaker rather than between speaker and auditor. Certainly this is the case in "Fra Lippo Lippi." Whether Lippo will extricate himself from the hands of the law is less important than how he will explain his conduct—both to himself and to the watchman. In "Bishop Blougram's Apology" Gigadibs is no match for the clever churchman, and the situation produced by the clash of the two men is less than dramatic. The real drama is within the Bishop.

In both poems, the auditor provides the speaker a stimulus for an *apologia pro vita sua* in which there are genuinely dramatic elements. He helps further to direct the speaker's self-exploration, and is sufficiently delineated to maintain the illusion of dramatic form. For him to participate more directly in the action would give to the monologue an emphasis other than that sought by the poet. "Saul" is another matter. Externally dramatic in form, it fails because neither speaker nor listener is clearly developed. Both lack reality—and the poem's diction, sentence structure, and rhythm are often mere "poeticalities," not functioning parts of a unified poem.

Realistic development of speaker, and, within the limits of his function, of the auditor, makes the poems both colloquial and dramatic. Whether or not Browning shares the views of Andrea, Lippo, or Bishop Blougram is unimportant, for in the poem ideas belong to the speaker and are expressed in his idiom. They are spoken to someone in the poem, not the reader. The dramatic illusion is partly sustained by cadence and syntax, embodying the speaker's experience and the ultimate expression of his personality and meaning.

Though other writers used the dramatic monologue before Browning, he, probably more than any other, established it as the preferred form for twentieth-century poets. Robinson and Frost, in their preoccupation with psychological explorations in the monologue form, have extended a tradition established by their nineteenth-century predecessor. Through Pound, who has often acknowledged his own indebtedness, Browning must also have influenced indirectly Eliot and others for whom Pound was long the accepted leader.[5]

To be sure, Browning's direct influence upon twentieth-century poets has been limited because, unlike Hopkins, his poetry was offered to a generation not prepared for it. At first he was misunderstood and rejected. Later, still misunderstood, he was enthusiastically accepted for the wrong things. Unfortunately also, Browning was not a sound critic of his own work, continuing to publish after his best poems had been written. It is interesting to conjecture what his influence might have been had that best been first published in 1918.

Browning's attempt to communicate dramatically the total experience of the speaker produces an unconventional syntax. Often the arrangement of the sentence is governed by the relative importance which the speaker attributes to its elements. He uses words associationally in thought and emotional groups so that distortion of syntax and omission of words—particularly of function words not ordinarily used in conversation—are inevitable. This makes many of his lines characteristically cryptic and elliptical. The effect is that of a mind in the act of communicating thought—thought that is emotional and sensuous.

Sometimes this practice, as in "The Bishop Orders His Tomb," for example, foreshadows the stream of consciousness technique. In such poems, words are used as symbols to communicate experiences in their preconscious, unformulated state. The unit of expression often becomes the single word, or the associational fragment; the unity is imaginative rather than grammatical.

In general, questions and exclamations are important structural forms, for both their nature and frequency portray character. Andrea shows frustration and fear in his timid, half-hearted questions. Both Lippo and Bishop Blougram, on the other hand, display intellectual acuteness and self-confidence in their forthright demands. Bishop Blougram's exclamations reflect self-confidence and beliefs positively held, the mark of punctuation coming as the inevitable termination of a statement forcefully made.

Browning avoids the end-stop line both rhetorically and rhythmically. Joining with the Romantics in their protest against the closed couplet, he went beyond any predecessor in his century by extending the run-on principle to include rhythm. Units begun in one line may be carried over and completed in the next, their length being determined by conversational cadence rather than traditional pattern. Browning, interested in the rhythm of the speaking voice, was careless of the musicality characteristic of much nineteenth-century verse.[6]

Metrically, he is in the tradition of Wyatt and Donne rather than that of Spenser and Tennyson. For like Wyatt's and Donne's, his lines give the impression of the speaking voice. The strong colloquial stress of key words and the irregular placement of beat prevent the reader from anticipating a predetermined pattern and focus attention upon the immediate word or word group.[7]

The kind of irregularity found in Wyatt, Donne,

and Browning—and in many of the twentieth-century poets—is more basic than that caused by the occasional shifting of stress primarily for variety or emphasis as in Shelley, Keats, and Tennyson—even in Pope. In these poets a basic rhythm is forcefully established, and the incidental irregularities come as mild surprises, as but temporary departures from the dominant rhythm. On the other hand, both Donne and Browning, ostensibly using the pentameter line, frequently take liberties with its length. Browning's blank verse lines vary from eight to fifteen syllables, making it impossible to anticipate a regular pattern such as characterizes even the most irregular of Tennyson's lines.

Sometimes Browning establishes the pentameter line and then superimposes upon it, counterpoint fashion, a four-beat line reminiscent of alliterative verse. This practice not only produces a variety, but provides an additional medium for expressing complex meaning: for example, it is one of the devices used to present the ʾversity-reconciliation theme in "Fra Lippo Lippi."

In turning from the part to the whole, we note that the effectiveness of Browning's monologues results primarily from a twofold accomplishment. The poet uses matter and structure with singleness of purpose to express a comprehensive mode of seeing; he succeeds in reconciling opposing forces so as to create unity, intensity, and vividness.

The unity of his poetry derives from a number of sources: it is partly material, partly structural. His skeptical approach, dialectical method, psychological alertness, and recurring patterns of thought and interest provide an organizing center for his work as a whole.

The singleness of his concept within the individual poem is further stabilized by his organic structural devices.

Browning's ability to maintain a consistency of tone in poems so different as "Bishop Blougram's Apology" and "Andrea del Sarto" is a psychological and artistic achievement. Sometimes one device becomes the chief, though never the only, means of drawing a poem together. In "Andrea del Sarto," symbol, precisely formulated and carefully controlled, is particularly effective. Both "Fra Lippo Lippi" and "Bishop Blougram's Apology" are unified by the coherency of an argument, which, characteristic of Browning's casuistic poems, serves purposes other than argumentative. Argument provokes character revelation and stimulates emotional reaction. In "Bishop Blougram's Apology" it serves as a dialectical drama which brings the poem into oneness. Browning's most characteristic and effective unifying device is irony. More than any other, it creates the tension found in all his best monologues. Particularly adapted to treating both conflict and multiple vision, it permits Browning to achieve unity without sacrificing his artistic detachment. Irony gives his work objectivity, complexity, intellectuality, intensity, seriousness, and humor, placing him in the "wit" rather than the "soul" tradition.

Browning's poetry as a whole is of uneven value. Much in the seventeen volumes which he wrote need not be salvaged, nor indeed, preserved. A considerable portion may be prized, not for its "philosophy" as the Browning societies would have it, but for its effectiveness in communicating a significant vision of life in a structure capable of stimulating diverse aesthetic responses. Browning's scope, intensity, and vividness assure his being read long after his early devotees have found other and more exciting inspiration for their "positive thinking."

Notes

I

ROBERT BROWNING'S APOLOGY

[1] For example: Rose Porter (compiler), *Bits of Burnished Gold* (New York: A. D. F. Randolph and Company, 1888); M. T. B., "Beautiful Bits for Busy Marthas," *Baptist Standard*, XXII (April, 1910), 18. Other choice bits include: Daniel Brinton, "Facettes of Love from Robert Browning," *Poet Lore*, I (1889), 1-27; "Helps to High Living," *Unity*, XXV (March 8, 1890), 15; W. D. W. Hyde, *The Art of Optimism as Taught by Robert Browning* (New York: Crowell, 1900); M. S. Dunn, "The Browning Tonic," *Atlantic Monthly*, XC (August, 1902), 203-11; John A. Hutton, *Guidance from Robert Browning in Matters of Faith* (Edinburgh: Oliphant, Anderson, and Ferrier, 1903); A. Rogers, *Prophecy and Poetry: Studies in Isaiah and Browning* (New York: Longmans, Green, 1909); Emily Hickey, "Glorious Robert Browning," *Nineteenth Century*, LXX (October, 1911), 753-70; John Powell, *Confessions of a Browning Lover* (New York: Abingdon Press, 1918).

[2] Ezra Pound, *Instigations* (New York: Boni and Liveright, 1920), pp. 123, 198, 199; *A B C of Reading* (New Haven: Yale University Press, 1934), pp. 162, 180; *Make It New* (London: Faber and Faber, 1934), pp. 146-50; *The Spirit of Romance* (New York: New Directions, n.d.), p. 132.

[3] Ford Madox Ford, *Thus to Revisit* (New York: E. P. Dutton and Co., 1921), p. 131.

[4] *Ibid.*, p. 133.

[5] *Ibid.*, p. 154.

[6] André Gide, *Journals*, Vol. III, trans. Justin O'Brien (New York: Alfred Knopf, 1949), p. 107.

[7] *Ibid.*, p. 335.

II

EVE AND THE VIRGIN

[1] William Empson, *Some Versions of Pastoral* (London: Chatto and Windus, 1935), p. 56.

III

SPORTIVE LADIES AND PATRON SAINT

[1] Ezra Pound, *ABC of Reading* (New Haven: Yale University Press, 1934), p. 128. This is essentially what Pound does say of *Sordello:* "It will be seen that the author is telling you something, not merely making a noise, he does not gum up the sound. The 'beauty' is not applied ornament, but makes the mental image more definite. The author is not hunting about for large high-sounding words, there is a very great variety in the rhyme but the reader runs on unaware." *Ibid.,* p. 180.

IV

ECCLESIASTICAL VISION IN STONE

[1] W. J. Rolfe and Heloise E. Hersey, *Selected Poems of Robert Browning* (New York: Harper and Brothers, 1886), p. 195.

[2] T. S. Eliot, *The Sacred Wood* (London: Methuen, 1920), pp. 116-17.

[3] T. S. Eliot, "The Metaphysical Poets," *Collected Essays* (New York: Harcourt, Brace and Company, 1932), p. 247.

V

SPIRITUAL DIALECTICS

[1] Stopford Brooke, *The Poetry of Robert Browning* (London: Isbister and Company, 1902), p. 394.

[2] Gilbert K. Chesterton, *Robert Browning* (London: Macmillan Company, 1903), p. 201.

[3] See: Mrs. Sutherland Orr, *A Handbook to the Works of Robert Browning* (London: George Bell and Sons, 1890), pp.

172-75; Edward Dowden, *Robert Browning* (London: J. M. Dent and Sons, 1915), pp. 199-202; Lafcadio Hearn, *Appreciations of Poetry* (New York: Dodd, Mead and Co., 1926), pp. 172-238; Lord Dunsany, "Browning Is Blougram," *Nineteenth Century*, CXXXIX (1946), 175-77; William O. Raymond, *The Infinite Moment* (Toronto: University of Toronto Press, 1950), pp. 122-55; Hoxie N. Fairchild, "Browning the Simplehearted Casuist," *University of Toronto Quarterly*, VIII (1949), 234-40; and for a position closer to mine here see: Arthur Symons, *An Introduction to the Study of Browning* (London: J. M. Dent and Co., 1906), pp. 111-12; C. R. Tracy, "Bishop Blougram," *Modern Language Review*, XXXIV (1939), 422-25; and especially F. E. L. Priestly, "Blougram's Apologetics," *University of Toronto Quarterly*, XV (1946), 139-47.

⁴ Browning acknowledged to Sir Charles Gavan Duffy that he had Cardinal Wiseman in mind when he wrote the poem, as indeed the Bishop's claim to having been born a Catholic would suggest. It is no more an accurate picture of Cardinal Wiseman, however, than "The Lost Leader" is of Wordsworth. There is much in the poem that is suggestive more of Cardinal Newman than of Cardinal Wiseman. Like Newman, Bishop Blougram is accused of dishonesty; he employs Newman's apologetic method, takes Newman's attitude toward liberalism and the miracles, and repeats some of his characteristic arguments in defense of the Church, insisting that Luther's "private judgment" leads to "the philosophy of Kant and the open infidelity of Strauss." See Newman's *Essays on Biblical and Ecclesiastical Miracles* (1843) and *Development of Christian Doctrine* (1845). Browning possibly had read these works and may have discussed them with his good friend, the ex-Jesuit, Father Prout, frequent visitor of the Brownings at the time "Bishop Blougram's Apology" was being written.

⁵ "Browning's Men and Women," *The Rambler*, V, n.s. (January, 1856), 54-71.

⁶ Browning often treats the ivory-tower idealist, and his attitude toward him is consistently unsympathetic. See especially: Arthur E. DuBois, "Robert Browning, Dramatist," *Studies in Philology*, XXXIII (1936), 626-55; Lionel Stevenson, "Tennyson, Browning and a Romantic Fallacy," *University of Toronto Quarterly*, XIII (1944), 175-95.

[7] Browning says he "bade the completest adieu" to English novelists on his first introduction to Balzac, "whom," he continues, "I greatly admire for his faculty, whatever he may choose to do with it." *The Letters of Robert Browning and Elizabeth Barrett Barrett, 1845-1846* (New York: Harper and Brothers, 1899), II, 107. In 1863 he referred to his "continuing passion" for *Madame Bovary.* Edward McAleer, ed., *Dearest Isa* (Austin: University of Texas Press, 1951), p. 173. See also remarks by Mrs. Browning in *The Letters of Elizabeth Barrett Browning*, ed. by F. G. Kenyon (London: Smith, Elder and Co., 1899), II, 304.

[8] Newman argues often from a position temporarily assumed. He had a keen understanding of the skeptical position, as he demonstrates in the memorandum "The Fluctuations of Human Opinion," printed in Wilfred Ward's *The Life of John Henry Cardinal Newman* (London: Longmans, Green, 1912), II, 242-43. He frequently formulated an argument only to refute it. Such is the case with his famous definition of a gentleman, so often assumed to be his own. Note the Bishop's use of similar technique particularly in lines 86, 161, 362, 387, 599, 647, 891. The fact that both Cardinal Newman and Bishop Blougram were probably expressing an undercurrent of skepticism which they had experienced in their own lives serves to make their technique even more effective.

[9] Joseph Baker, in *Pippa Passes and Shorter Poems* (New York: The Odyssey Press, 1947, p. 353) calls attention to the contrast between the Bishop's certitude and that of St. Thomas, quoting the following from the official philosopher of the Church: ". . . the intellect assents to something, not through being sufficiently moved to this assent by its proper object, but through an act of choice, whereby it turns voluntarily to one side rather than the other: and if this be accompanied by doubts and fears of the opposite side, there will be opinion, while, if there be certainty, and no fear of the opposite side, there will be faith." *Summa Theologica*, II-II, Q. i, A. 4, tr. by Fathers of the English Dominican Province (London: 1917), pp. 9-10.

[10] Thomas Carlyle, "Characteristics," *Collected Works*, "Centenary Edition" (New York: Charles Scribner's Sons, 1896-99), XXVIII, 11. Browning's early enthusiasm for Carlyle was pronounced, but with the years a breach, intellectual, if not per-

sonal, developed between the two men. In 1846 Browning said of Carlyle, "I love him enough not to envy him nor wish to change places. . . ." *The Letters of Robert Browning and Elizabeth Barrett*, I, 380. By 1857 he was "cursing and swearing" over *Frederick*. *Dearest Isa*, ed. by Edward McAleer (Austin: The University of Texas Press, 1951), p. 35. William Clyde DeVane has brilliantly discussed "The Parleying with George Bubb Doddington" (1887) as an answer to Carlyle's gloomy philosophy. *Browning's Parleyings* (New Haven: Yale University Press, 1927), pp. 134-66.

[11] For statements of poetic intention, unusual from Browning, who consistently refused to discuss his own works, see a series of letters concerning *The Ring and the Book* in *Robert Browning and Julia Wedgwood*, ed. by Richard Curle (New York: Frederick Stokes and Co., 1937), pp. 138-78.

VI

SPIRITUAL DOGMATICS

[1] Arthur Symons, *An Introduction to the Study of Browning* (London: J. M. Dent and Company, 1906), p. 89.

[2] Anna M. Stoddart, "Saul," *Browning Society Papers*, II, 264-68.

[3] Edith C. Batho and Bonamy Dobrée, *The Victorians and After* (New York: Robert M. McBride and Company, 1938), p. 50.

[4] *The Shorter Poems of Robert Browning*, ed. by William C. DeVane (New York: F. S. Croft and Company, 1936), p. 359.

[5] *The Letters of Robert Browning and Elizabeth Barrett Barrett* (New York: Harper and Brothers, 1899), I, 2.

[6] Betty Miller, *Robert Browning: A Portrait* (London: John Murray, 1952), p. 178.

[7] William Empson, *Some Versions of Pastoral* (London: Chatto and Windus, 1935), especially pages 206-7, 260-61.

[8] *The Letters of Robert Browning and Elizabeth Barrett Barrett*, I, 178-79.

[9] See particularly W. R. Inge, "The Mysticism of Robert Browning," *Studies of English Mystics* (London: John Murray, 1906); Caroline F. E. Spurgeon, *Mysticism in English Literature* (Cambridge: At the University Press, 1913).

[10] Browning later was to condemn severely the rococo style of some of his contemporaries. He referred to Swinburne's poetry as a "fuzz of words," "florid impotence, to my taste—the *minimum* of thought and idea in the *maximum* of words and phraseology"; to Rossetti's as "*scented* with poetry, as it were—like trifles of various sorts you take out of a cedar or sandalwood box"; to Victor Hugo's as "one big bubble of mere breath which a touch breaks—in turning over the leaves of the book itself: . . . he can't let the truth be truth, or a number of remarkable poetical pieces speak for themselves, without assuring you that he meant them to join Man to God, with like pleasant practicalities." *Letters of Robert Browning*, ed. by Thurman L. Hood (London: John Murray, 1933), pp. 54, 136, 137.

[11] For her numerous suggestions for changes in the meter of the poem see Frederick G. Kenyon, "Miss Elizabeth Barrett-Barrett's Criticism of Some of Her Future Husband's Poems (1845)," *New Poems by Robert Browning and Elizabeth Barrett Browning* (New York: Macmillan and Co., 1915), pp. 157-61.

[12] René Wellek and Austin Warren, *Theory of Literature* (New York: Harcourt Brace and Co., 1949), p. 126. Wellek goes on to say: "Yet blurred outlines, vagueness of meaning, and illogicality are not, in a literal sense, 'musical' at all."

VII

THE BOW AND THE LYRE

[1] William Empson, *Some Versions of Pastoral* (London: Chatto and Windus, 1935), p. 54.

[2] T. S. Eliot, *John Dryden* (New York: Terence and Elsa Holliday, 1932), pp. 12-14; *The Use of Poetry and the Use of Criticism* (London: Faber and Faber, 1933), pp. 67-81.

[3] F. L. Lucas, *Ten Victorian Poets* (Cambridge: At the University Press, 1940), p. 25.

[4] B. W. A. Massey, *Browning's Vocabulary: Compound Epithets* (Poznau: Dawniej Fiszer, 1931), pp. 38-39.

[5] Pound places at least a part of Eliot's poetry in the tradition of *Men and Women*. *Instigations* (New York: Boni and Liveright, 1920), p. 199.

[6] Browning was criticized adversely by most of his con-

temporaries for his metrical irregularities. Tennyson refused to read *The Ring and the Book* because he could not "put up with obsolete horrors, and unrhythmical composition" through a "volume of spasms." Hallam Tennyson, *Tennyson and His Friends* (London: Macmillan Company, 1911), pp. 51-52. Carlyle preferred Tennyson's style to Browning's, saying, "Alfred knows how to jingle, but Browning does not." William M. Rossetti, *Pre-Raphaelite Diaries and Letters* (London: Hurst and Blackett, 1900), p. 304. Henry James referred to him as a poet "without a lyre." Henry James, "Browning in Westminster Abbey," *Essays in London and Elsewhere* (New York: Harpers, 1893), p. 226. Francis Thompson said that in his poetry there were "no harmonies" but only "roughness like the roughness of a harsh male voice." Francis Thompson, "Academy Portrait XXVI," reprinted in *Literary Criticism by Francis Thompson,* ed. by Terence L. Connolly (New York: E. P. Dutton and Company, 1948), pp. 148-49.

[7] Arnold Stein has called such movement "vertical." "Horizontal rhythm," on the other hand, constitutes a regular pattern which, easily anticipated, offers less impediment to a direct forward movement of the line. "Structure of Sound in Donne's Verse," *Kenyon Review,* XIII (Winter and Spring, 1951), 20-36, 256-78.

Index

SELECTED ANN ARBOR PAPERBACKS

works of enduring merit

PB 21575

For a complete list of Ann Arbor Paperback titles write:

THE UNIVERSITY OF MICHIGAN PRESS / ANN ARBOR